John Rogers, S Penson

Guide Book & Atlas of Muskoka and Parry Sound Districts

John Rogers, S Penson

Guide Book & Atlas of Muskoka and Parry Sound Districts

ISBN/EAN: 9783741118845

Manufactured in Europe, USA, Canada, Australia, Japa

Cover: Foto ©Thomas Meinert / pixelio.de

Manufactured and distributed by brebook publishing software (www.brebook.com)

John Rogers, S Penson

Guide Book & Atlas of Muskoka and Parry Sound Districts

Guide Book & Atlas

of Muskoka and Parry Sound Districts

MAPS BY Jno ROGERS

TORONTO
H.R. PAGE & Co

SKETCHES BY S. PENSON

Entered According to the Act of the Parliament of Canada, in the Year One Thousand Eight Hundred and Seventy Nine by H.R.Page & Co in the office of the Minister of Agriculture.

LIST OF POST OFFICES.

EXPLANATIONS.

School House...................
Church ....
Saw Mill ....
Grist Mill ....
House.........................
Hotel ....
Store ....

MUSKOKA

AND

PARRY SOUND DISTRICTS.

By W. E. HAMILTON, Esq.

INTRODUCTORY.

The free grant districts of Muskoka and Parry Sound are, year by year, exciting fuller and deeper interest, not only in the older settlements of Ontario but throughout the sister provinces of the Dominion, the United States and Europe.

In addition to what may be called the emigrating class (embracing all ranks and grades of society, from the richest to the poorest, and from the most highly cultivated down to the illiterate peasant) another very important and increasing multitude make Muskoka their temporary home—we mean the tourists, those birds of passage, who, like the swallows, annually cool themselves by a migration to our northern fastnesses, and depart refreshed. There are also hunters, and trappers, and anglers, and many other unclassified travellers, who visit Muskoka in ever increasing numbers. All these visitors with one consent cry out, "Give us maps, give us something descriptive of Muskoka to guide us before we start for the North, and to retain as a *souvenir* of our journey." The emigration agent in Bracebridge, Mr. W. E. Hamilton, reports a continual stream of such applicants for maps and descriptive matter in Muskoka, while the Crown Lands agent, Mr. A. White, is similarly beseiged.

The publication of the present atlas is designed to satisfy these urgent demands of land seekers, immigrants and tourists, by giving them a trustworthy series of maps, one of which embraces the whole free grant territory, while the various townships are also mapped separately. These maps have been lithographed from original drawings made by Mr. John Rogers and his assistants, who personally traversed the whole ground and revised and corrected the government surveys, adding much topographical detail which was not given in the former maps. The survey involved much personal fatigue and labor; the result is now before the public. The govern-

ment township maps were of far less use to the land seeker than they might have been, because the roads were not plotted on them, and therefore as an itinerary to the settler they were useless.

This deficiency has been here supplied, and the land hunter can map out his journey before leaving Bracebridge, Rosseau or Parry Sound, as the case may be, to his future home. In addition to the government roads, the statute labor roads are also given. Drawings from the pencil of Mr. S. Penson, an accomplished artist, are also presented, of the places of interest in the districts, or rather let us say, of the conjoint district, which in this introduction we shall henceforth, for shortness and to avoid cumbrous phraseology, call MUSKOKA—a name already so applied for electoral purposes, with the same advantage of brevity.

The maps, prepared regardless of expense and revised with frequent and minute scrutiny, speak for themselves; so far from their being subordinate or auxiliary to the descriptive matter, the latter is to be taken by the reader as subsidiary to the atlas proper. He should not, therefore, expect an elaborate treatise on Muskoka, which would have enormously increased the cost of the atlas without any proportionate boon to the public. Yet it is hoped that what follows will not only interest the reader's attention but aid him to realize what sort of a country he is about to visit. All available sources of information (whether the files of living and extinct journals, the letters and oral jottings of settlers, or the pages of the "Undeveloped Portions of Ontario," published by Messrs. Kirkwood & Murphy, of Toronto) have been utilized, and no pains have been spared to expunge errors wherever detected. In the composition of the work the difficulty has been altogether out of proportion to its bulk, when printed. When the author traversed ground outside his own personal knowledge he was obliged to go over huge piles of printed matter and MSS. with a view to pick the solitary grain of wheat out of much chaff. Should any local or other reader detect some error, he or she will confer a favor on the author by communicating it to him for correction in subsequent editions of this work.

Muskoka (which term also embraces Parry Sound, in this connection) has for its principal boundaries the Bobcaygeon Road on the east, the Georgian Bay on the west, Lake Nipissing and French River on the north, and the Severn River on the south. Our neighbors, therefore, are the older settled portions of the counties of Simcoe and Victoria, a portion of the county of Peterborough, and Algoma. On the north there seems to be no bar to our ultimate advancement till we reach a climate too cold and in too high a latitude for agriculture, and it is well known that most excellent land lies on the north of Lake Nipissing. The extent (as computed from the areas of the various surveyed townships in Muskoka and Parry Sound given in the "Undeveloped Lands of Ontario") is 5,500 square miles, but taking in unsurveyed townships and considering the ultimate territorial heritage of our people, we may call the area of Muskoka (used in the broad sense of the term) 10,000 square miles. Let us follow the track of our representative in the Local House, Mr. J. C. Miller, who, in the course of a very telling speech on Muskoka, compared our infant settlement territorially with some of the ancient kingdoms of Europe, and also with American States or provinces. Aiding ourselves by a table kindly furnished by his son (Upper Canada College), we see that the free grant districts are, in round numbers, five times as large as either the Province of Prince Edward's Island in our Dominion, or Delaware in the United States; five times the size of Connecticut; one-fifth larger than New Jersey or Massachusett; within one-eleventh of the size of Belgium; lacking a sixth of the extent of Holland; and a third of that of Denmark or Switzerland.

The comparative statistics of these old settled countries cannot be dismissed without a glance at their respective populations, as forecasting the future vital density of Muskoka, and the numerical limit to which we may aspire within the sober bounds of reasonable hope. Taking the limiting extremes of density of population among the nations, states and provinces above cited, we find that our free grant districts could sustain 460,000 people judged by the standard of Prince Edward's Island, or 4,400,000 judged by that of Belgium. The intermediate returns from Switzerland and Denmark would suggest populations of 1,670,000 and 1,200,000 respectively. My estimate, therefore (published two years ago in the "Undeveloped Lands of Ontario"), of 100,000 souls, whereof 80,000 should live by agriculture, and 20,000 by manufacturing, commerce and other pursuits, as the population which we might ultimately reach, is within a safe margin of sober forecast. We *are* reach-

ing that limit by gigantic strides. Fourteen years ago a small church would have held all the people from the Severn to the Georgian Bay; seven years later we could have filled Spurgeon's Tabernacle, now we outnumber the white population of British Columbia. The quotations of experts place the present population of these free grant districts between 26,000 and 30,000. The writer leans more to the choice of the latter than the former figure. In his published estimate (two years ago) he called the population "over 20,000." Remembering the large intervening immigration, and guided by the returns of the number of qualified electors at the recent general election, he rather leans to the number 30,000 as our present limit. The district is so rapidly filling up as to necessitate a quinquennial census. We shall not, however, have long to wait for the next decennial enumeration, and 1881 will show the free grant system to have been a pronounced success. Among the minor curiosities of our census may be mentioned the possession of pagan Indians, real *bona fide* and tolerably picturesque pagans in the Parry Sound district. As to the distribution of our people by nationalities, we are thoroughly mixed. We have pioneers from almost every country in Europe, except Turkey, the British Isles being our main feeders, though we have a respectable German and Scandinavian contingent. This year it is to be hoped that a vigorous effort will be made to divert a fair share of the Mennonite immigration to Muskoka. In addition, we have of course large numbers of native Canadians, not excluding those born in Muskoka, which swell our ranks in ever increasing numbers, the average of five to a family being ludicrously below the mark in Muskoka. Until lately, take of English, Irish, Scotch equal parts, sift thoroughly and add a dose of Canadians equal to the whole, would have been a good recipe to get at our Muskoka mixture. Taking up a voter's list at random, it would now be an even bet whether the name of a given man was Canadian or from the British Isles. We have also a sprinkling of intelligent Americans and would like more. Within the last three years the immigration has shown a preponderating Canadian element.

Reader, do you want to know first what sort of looking country Muskoka is? If you could get a bird's eye view of the region from a balloon soaring over the centre, you would see between the Severn River and the Georgian Bay, and stretching northward to Lake Nipissing, a land of forests seamed with open spaces where the axe had let in the light of day, with large clearings free from stumps in its older parts, and increasing inroads even in the forest of its northern fringes. From that towering height the rock would not obtrude itself strongly on the view: a peculiarity of Muskoka rock, as compared for instance with that of the three kingdoms, being the facility with which trees find foothold in the most tiny crevices, and the rapidity with which they clothe the naked crag. But till you soar above the region of cloud land, one great "thing of beauty" and joy to the husbandman, a countless chain of lakes, would gleam here, there and everywhere, pitting the surface of the land with liquid mirrors of every conceivable shape and contortion of outline. Muskoka is eminently *lake land*, a more descriptive name, we must confess, than the "clear sky land," now immortalized in the pages of *All the Year Round*.

Some of these lakes form a connected chain of navigable waters, and others are isolated; while some few seem to have no outlet nor any supply from rivers, being fed, no doubt, mainly by underground springs. They vary in size from a tiny pond, which is only a lake by courtesy, to the huge proportions of Lake Nipissing. Some, resembling Muskoka Lake, are dark from some unexplained cause, and others (the Lake of Bays and Lake Joseph for instance) are clear and limpid. They are generally deep, and almost always surrounded by a wall of dark green foliage, unbroken except by clearings or by the occasional intrusion of rock. The larger lakes are full of islands, Muskoka Lake being popularly said to have an island for every day in the year. Such islands occasionally, in their turn, contain miniature lakes. A very large proportion of the islands in our front lakes (Muskoka, Rosseau, and Joseph) have been bought by wealthy tourists from the "front," as places of summer residence, and on several of these charming sites handsome villas will be built, Judge Gowan, of Barrie, being about to set the example on Eilian Gowan Island. The number of the Muskoka and Parry Sound lakes is very great, and far exceeds that indicated by the government maps, which only show those encountered in running what may be called the skeleton lines of the survey. There can hardly be less than 600 altogether, and, according to the official returns, they occupy at least *one-tenth* of the whole area of Muskoka and Parry Sound, the Township of Humphrey having almost exactly one-fourth of its area consisting of water, while the water-area of Himsworth is only one in every thirteen hundred acres. Our lakes abound with fish, and their banks with game and fur bearing animals. Even where they are not traversed by steamboats, these lakes form in many cases a very convenient mode of transit from settlement to settlement. Innumerable varieties of nautical architecture dot our waters—dug-out canoes, clumsy and slow, but capacious to hold merchandise, and un-capsizable; bark canoes, swift, graceful, and most trying to the nerves of the uninitiated; sail-boats and lap-streak row boats; scows for the carriage of hay and lumbermen's supplies; the raft of lumber with its floating shanty, and other

specimens not enumerated. One result is that many of our Muskoka people, young and old, male and female, are good canoeists, and lead an amphibious life for a large portion of the year. In the winter, when a lake has been thoroughly frozen, it forms a splendid level and direct sleigh-road from point to point, though during recent winters, owing to the ice having been pressed down by superabundant snow before it had gained strength and thickness, these lake sleigh roads have often turned out to be only sloppy deceptions.

Another and a most important use of these lakes, is to temper the climate, and very sensibly moderate the otherwise injurious effects of frost. It is easy to see that a territory, flanked so largely on one boundary by the inland sea of the Georgian Bay, and having at least one-tenth of its surface filled by widely distributed lakes, must be cooler in summer and less injured by frost at all times, unless in the very depth of winter, than a country lacking lakes.

In fact, to speak popularly, the frost has extra work to do, in freezing these lakes first, and thus the arrival of its undisputed sway is delayed. Again, the moist air from so large a body of interspersed lakes prevents summer droughts, while it protects the soil, very largely from the action of summer frosts, the incidence of which has not been felt seriously in Muskoka.

Lastly, these lakes serve as reservoirs to receive, and gradually give forth, the tribute of violent floods, which otherwise would inundate the low-lying lands and valleys adjacent to rivers, carrying havoc into many a home, and sweeping the garnered grain before them in their ruthless torrent.

On Muskoka rivers it is unnecessary to dilate largely in this place. An instance of one navigable for the largest class of steamers which can twist in and out through its puzzling sinuosities, can be seen in the Muskoka river, from the lake of the same name, to Bracebridge. There is depth enough for the largest steamer which the necessities of our increasing commerce can ever call for; but the continual changes of direction require first-class steering, especially for a long steamer like the Nipissing or the Wenonah, the former of which can just turn round at the Bracebridge wharf on her return journey. Under the experienced pilotage, however, of Mr. Cockburn's captains, who know every nook and corner of the river as well as I know my office pigeonholes, the voyage is safe and speedy. The action of the wash from the waves generated by the steamers, together with the natural friction of the current and violent abrasion in flood time, have combined to wear away the banks of the river, and it is a matter of surprise that the riparian proprietors have not long since sought a remedy by planting willows or otherwise arresting the encroachments of the water on their river frontage. This portion of the Muskoka river is most admirably suited for a most extensive carrying trade, Nature having already done the work of fully deepening its channel, a work effected on the Clyde by artificial means, at an expenditure of millions of dollars.

The Magnetewan is also navigable by steamers, but as a rule the Muskoka rivers are very much broken by rapids or waterfalls, though the connecting links of smooth water are generally navigable. The future will see these rapids evaded by tramway portages, or boldly defied by the construction of locks; but to us of the present age they say, "thus far shalt thou go and no further." The Muskoka river, when ascended from the lake, is found to branch into two separate rivers, one being called the "South Branch" and the other the "North Branch." Each of these is broken by a series of unnavigable rapids. The South Branch forms the connecting link between Muskoka Lake and the Lake of Bays, Trading Lake, and a whole family of small adjacent lakes and lakelets. The North Branch proceeds from the navigable chain of Mary, Fairy, and Vernon Lakes.

It is hard to say where the "river" ends, and the "creek" begins, in the descending catalogue, and a similar difficulty besets one who would try to difference a small lake from a large pond. In fact "creeks," as we call them here, and hardly worthy of a name, would be historic rivers in Europe, sanctified by the genius of Scott, Byron or Wordsworth, and echoing in the household speech of millions of firesides, where the deathless poet had brought such spots vividly before the stranger's eye in all their matchless beauty. Muskoka abounds with countless creeks, some few vanishing in the height of summer, but the vast majority sparkling permanently and with but slightly varying volume.

Now, gentle reader, I must bring you to something on which all the abusive epithets in the English language have been poured out in lavish abundance, a hard, rugged, undeniable fact—the Muskoka rock. It is unfortunate that Muskoka, geologically, does not "put its best leg foremost," to use the old proverbial advice, but, on the contrary, seems to awe the would-be agriculturist, whether he enter the territory from Parry Sound or from Washago, by showing him the upland ground-floor of primeval rocks. He stands appalled. Committing the traveller's error denounced by Archbishop Whately, of too hasty generalization, and assuming that he sees but a prelude to an unbroken sea of rocks, his dismal wail rings about : "How can I sow or reap on these crags? Where can I even coax a scanty pasture for the hardiest sheep?" The immortal allegory is realized in our Muskoka pilgrim. The giant Maul appears to test him. Feeble-minded and Ready-to-halt are paralysed, while

Great-Heart goes on to conquer. Let us comfort the stranger. These rocky barriers, which fringe our territory and frown on the incomer, are *not* true samples of Muskoka land. This fact can be studied very well in Bracebridge. The rock crops out at the right bank of the river, between the Falls and the wharf, and elsewhere occasionally within the village limits, but the level plain beyond the intersection of Dominion and Manitoba streets is some forty feet deep, the top-soil being of all varieties, from a sandy soil to clay, but very largely consisting of a rich clay loam, eighteen inches or two feet deep, without a stone or pebble.

The same variety of soil is observable all over Muskoka, and one comforting peculiarity of the Muskoka rock is its abruptly jutting nature—steeply ascending from the ground, steeply descending below it. As the same rock on the lake shore dips so rapidly that deep anchorage is afforded within immediate reach of land, so, in the soil, anchorage rich and deep for plant-roots is found so close to the rock, that splendid corn often rubs its pendent leaves against the stony wall. Many farmers have noticed that the best soil is near the rock, without knowing the reason, which is probably due to a weathering of the feldspathic portion, which yields comminuted plant-food in a very available form.

The rock is also a wonderful store-house for heat, and a reservoir of moisture, which it gives out in time of summer dryness. It also serves to break the winds in all directions, and furnish a building material for houses, drains, fences, &c., which will be more and more utilized. Flat rock is rare, and so are field-stones, which, even in some parts of the three kingdoms, crop up in working land which was ploughed in the days of Julius Cæsar. A sufficient proof of the moist nature of the Muskoka rock is given by the healthy growth thereupon of the cypress and other trees, whose *habitat* is usually in swamps. Instances are common of large pine trees growing on the bare rock, and showing their hugh naked roots twining round it, and firmly wedged in some moist cleft of the crag.

It is difficult to give an average of the proportion of good land in the districts, but we are not over-shooting the mark in calling it 60 per cent. And be it remembered that the rejected 40 per cent. includes swamps, many of which, at a trifling cost, could be reclaimed so as to make the most valuable portions of the farm. Even the rocky portion of this 40 per cent. is by no means absolute rock; much of it would make excellent sheep-pastures, though too broken to be ploughed. And the Ontario Government, in the case of a single man, makes an additional Free Grant to cover the rock and swamp, so that he shall have 100 acres of cultivable land, altogether.

The Muskoka rock resembling granite, and called " gneiss," geologically, is, like the former, a compound of three distinct substances—quartz, mica and granite. Sometimes one of these elements is found predominating or alone, and thus we have quartz seams, feldspathic rock, or stones which are almost pure mica. This " gneiss " rock is the most abundant in the Muskoka district, but there are varieties of allied rocks associated with it, and, though the mineral exploration of Muskoka can hardly be said to be commenced, yet a beginning has been made, sufficient to inspire hope of future commercial returns. Gold has been found in the nugget form, though of small size, in Gravenhurst and in the Township of Stevenson. A small nugget from the former locality was examined by the writer, and found to be, undoubtedly, the royal metal, in considerable purity. The discovery was made accidentally, in the *debris* of excavated earth from a well in Gravenhurst, by Mr. Neil Livingstone, in the spring of 1877. This gold was sometimes imbedded in fragments of rock, and sometimes free. Gold also in the solid rock has been worked near Rosseau.

Gold-bearing pyrites, and some very pure samples of iron ore, may also be included in the list of minerals. The writer has in his possession a sample of iron ore, from Stisted, which Prof. Croft, of Toronto, was kind enough to analyze, and pronounced to consist of almost chemically pure iron, with a trace of manganese. He is also indebted to Prof. Croft for the analysis of a mineral which had all the appearance of plumbago, but which turned out to be molybdenite. Indeed, the Professor has, most liberally and promptly, responded on several occasions to requests for information as to Muskoka minerals. Geologists can only overcome the proverbial difficulty of " proving a negative" as to Muskoka minerals, in the case of coal, and no doubt probably lignite, the absence of which we must except as a finality. As to plumbago, manganese, and a host of other minerals, such a large area of the Muskoka rock is covered by forests, that he must be a rash prophet who would venture to deny the possibility or even likelihood of their discovery after large clearings become the rule, and the attention both of our own people and of outsiders has been turned to explore the bowels of the earth for the treasures which underlie the barren places of its surface.

Even as to the existence, at some future time, of gold in paying quantities in Muskoka, nothing negative can be inferred by any but the flimsiest reasoner from the failure to find a paying gold-field at Gravenhurst by the simple process of random well-digging. The accidental discovery of Gravenhurst gold was useless without a combination of capital and scientific skill to develop the treasure. Both were lacking. If an expert had been called in to trace the exact bed-plane and winding of the gravel where the nugget had been discovered, and to determine whether an infiltration from Gull Lake might not have caused a subterranean channel to the lower water, along the course of which channel an accumulation of the precious metal could be looked for—a very different sequel might have been ours to record to-day. None of these things seem to have been thought of; the delving and washing ended—as all such unscientific and blindfold efforts generally end—in failure. Many had the most absurd ideas about this gold field. They heard that gold had been found in Gravenhurst in a certain well; they rushed out per N. R. R., asked peremptorily for the visible nuggets, sternly peered into the ground with magnifying glasses, and, having found nothing yellow or glittering, voted Gravenhurst a fraud, and every one connected with Muskoka an embryo Barnum. Such simpletons from the front were to be seen thronging the Gravenhurst hotels during the gold excitement in 1877. More intelligent observers washed a panful of the gravel, found that a little heavier residuum was found in the bottom of the pan, dried it and examined it with a magnifying glass, found no yellow grains therein, and voted the Gravenhurst Ophir a delusion. The delusion sprung from the ignorance of these explorers as to the simplest facts and principles of gold mining. The non-appearance of visible gold (whether in nuggets or otherwise) is no proof whatever of the unprofitable nature of a gold field. All that glitters is not gold, and some things which do not glitter contain it. Yellow mica and iron or copper-pyrites, have often deceived the greenhorn, while Dana, in p. 321 of his " Mineralogy," tells us that " Masses of quartz, with no external indications of gold, examined in the above way [crushing and hand-panning], afforded an average of more than eight dollars to the bushel of gold rock." Dr. Dawson, Principal of McGill College, Montreal, in his "Acadian Geology," 2nd edition, p. 625, says : "The gold deposits of the river Chaudière, in Lower Canada, afford another instance in which, while individual search has proved quite unprofitable, washing operations on a large scale, with the aid of machinery, have repaid the capital employed. * * *" [P. 629] "Those veins and parts of veins which contain many 'sights' or visible portions of gold, are less rich in disseminated gold than those which are deficient in visible gold. Some of the richest veins, indeed, rarely show visible gold, while others which contain nuggets are, in other respects, very poor." Indeed, when we think, as Dr. Dawson has well suggested, of the millions of quartz-veins intersecting the rocks of a granite country, combined with the fact that perhaps only one in a million of these is gold-bearing, the wonder is, not that so few gold-veins are discovered, but that discoveries are ever made, more especially in a new country like Muskoka, where the bush hides its mineral treasures. Capital and patience are both needed; no hasty explorations will suffice. The discoverer of the rich Wine Harbor deposit in Nova Scotia spent two years in finding out that gold deposit. One encouraging feature of future gold explorations in Muskoka, is the aid furnished to the modern miner by the gigantic strides of chemical discovery. The chlorine process extracts gold from 10,000 times its weight of poor materials, and the still more important discovery of the sodium-quicksilver amalgam utilizes rejected tailings of deserted claims. Poor sands and rock which would have been scornfully rejected twenty years ago can be now made to pay.

Passing back from gold to the baser metals, we see that the presence of iron is very marked throughout the free grant districts, so much so as occasionally to puzzle surveyors by local attraction of their magnetic needles, and there seems nothing to forbid the manufacture of steel ingots out of the pure iron ore, recently described, by the aid of charcoal made from adjacent hard wood. Such an industry has been profitable even under the hands of Hindoos and savage Maoris. The metallurgy and mineral future of Muskoka is full of hope. Without delaying to glance at the discovery of yellow ochre in Bracebridge, let us record the presence, in certain localities (the Parry Sound Road, Magnetewan, and on the shores of Whitestone Lake), of limestone. Imported rock lime, though its price has been reduced from 55c. to 29c. per bushel in Bracebridge, must always be expensive by reason of the heavy freight. It is satisfactory to know, therefore, that such limestone centres exist to supply circles, the radii of which extend so far that the advantage in freight practically excludes the imported article. The native limestone is crystallized, in fact at Whitestone Lake and Hagerman, there is a smooth and beautiful rock, owned by Mr. G. Kelsey, near the Narrows, which has all the appearance of the whitest Carrara marble, though its coarser texture is said to bar its use to supersede ordinary marble. The native lime is much stronger than the imported and will bear a far larger addition of sand. At the time of the writer's residence near Whitestone Lake, the result of the burning was very inferior to what it might have been, owing to the clumsy construction of the kilns, and the ignorance, on the part of their owners, as to the proper mode of burning and even slacking this peculiar limestone.

The thanks of all concerned in the Atlas are due to various officials and others, who have aided the work. Messrs. J. Ewart Lount (Registrar), Aubrey White (Crown Land Agent), in Bracebridge; Messrs. Frank Foley and Thomas McMurray, occuping similar positions in Parry Sound; William Beatty, Esq., Parry Sound;

James Boyer, village clerk, Bracebridge; D. Patterson, township clerk, McKellar; D. F. Macdonald, Parry Sound; George Kelsey, Dunchurch; C. Rumball, Port Sydney; T. M. Robinson, Gravenhurst; James Sharpe, inspector of weights and measures, Gravenhurst; John Toye, township clerk, Ryde, and Fred. Richardson, township clerk, Watt, are especially to be thanked. If some localities have been less perfectly described than others, the fault has been with their township clerks and other prominent men, who failed to respond to the request for information, which was published (giving ample time for reply) in the columns of the *Free Grant Gazette*.

SCENERY.

To the artistic eye of the traveller who hungers after tit-bits of forest vistas, and thirsts for glimpses of far-off and half-concealed islands, Muskoka is a thing of beauty and a joy not soon to be forgotten.

With the exception of the lakes traversed by Mr. A. P. Cockburn's steamers, Muskoka is a virgin field for the great army of tourists. A few skirmishers may have ventured up to Mary Lake, or Baysville, but to the majority Muskoka means—Pratt's Hotel at Rosseau, or Fraser's of Port Cockburn, and the adjacent islands.

Even Bracebridge they only know, if at all, by the rocks which flank a portion of its harbor. Perhaps they never leave the deck of the steamer, as she touches at the village landing-place, and they see nothing of the business streets of the village itself, or of the beautiful waterfalls which lie within an hour's drive of its limits. Still less do they know of Mary, Fairy, and Vernon Lakes, that beautiful chain of connected waters, now so accessible, and traversed by a commodious steamer, or the Lake of Bays, with its sinuous contortions and pine-clad peninsulas, which this year ('78) have had their echoes, for the first time, awakened by the steamboat's whistle.

Bracebridge is eminently the natural centre for tourists who wish to see the Muskoka waterfalls, with a minimum expenditure of time and money. The three largest, and one of the smaller of these numerous falls, can be seen easily in one day by the tourist to whom economy of time is an object. Not the least attractive cascade (60 feet in descent) is in the heart of the village of Bracebridge. The summer tourist, standing on the bridge which spans the cataract, sees, at one glance, the Bracebridge Fall, and the two dark and smooth bodies of water which precede and follow it. On one side of the bridge the placid and unrippled water flows under a lofty and curving plateau crowned with villas, and sloping down near the bridge to a little gem of green prairie darkened by the shade of over-hanging pines. Perhaps a floating leaf may aid the stranger to realize the treacherous swiftness

SOUTH FALLS, MUSKOKA RIVER.

of the current as it approaches the upper side of the abutments of the bridge. Turning from this glimpse of lake-like placidity, let the tourist step to the south-western hand-rail of the bridge, and find a transformation effected. Glassy stillness and gloomy darkness of water are succeeded by white sparkling foam, and the turmoil of the fretted element, in all its "tempestuous loveliness." Water in every conceivable shape and contortion is here; sometimes thundering over some jutting crag which has defied its power from century to century, or again striking against a hidden splinter of gneiss, and throwing up a fountain of foam and spray to sparkle in the summer sun. The gradations of color in the water vary from the sombre and almost stygian tint of the Muskoka river, in its normal state, to absolute whiteness, according as it is more or less furiously pulverized by its impact on the rocky bed of the torrent.

The rocks, during a portion of the descent, show a smooth, sloping plane, while elsewhere they are irregular and shapeless crags. Everywhere the dark, and sometimes ferruginous, color gives a sombre setting to the succession of white foaming leaps by which the north branch of the Muskoka River at length gains the peaceful and oval basin of the Bracebridge Harbor.

The summer scene is often very striking from this side of the bridge. Beyond the basin or harbor, on the left bank, lies a dark, pine forest, while the opposite side is rocky near the water's edge, and sandy beach. The blue curl of a smoke-wreath moves along and between the trees, tracing the course of the incoming steamer as she nears the harbor. Steamer and river are alike invisible to the gazer from the bridge, till at length the graceful "Nipissing" disgorges her living freight at the wharf.

Other aspects are presented by the Bracebridge Falls, when butterflies and summer birds have given way to snow-flakes, and when the white foam of the falls is eclipsed by the yet more dazzling whiteness of snow-clad ice banks, which, gradually growing as winter progresses, finally all but meet over the water's edge.

In spring, the water is at its highest, and thousands of logs come thundering over the basin, which is finally so filled that an active man can walk across the floating floor from bank to bank. Some idea of the terrific power of the water forces itself on the spectator's mind when he sees a huge log which a yoke of oxen could scarcely move dashed like a feather from rock to rock, and sometimes split into pieces with the resistless thud of the concussion.

So much for the Bracebridge Falls on the north branch of the Muskoka River. Let us ascend this branch, passing minor falls, till, at a distance of about four miles, we reach the High Falls. In the dry season this fall (or rather assemblage of falls, for the total volume of water is divided into three separate falls by two islands) is best approached from the right bank, whence the "gorge" can be seen in full operation, while the two other falls are insignificant images of their volume in the season of flood. The scenery through which the traveller walks in reaching the right bank of the falls is very peculiar, and rather different from what he might anticipate. Unless just at the water's edge, very little rock is visible during the ascent; on the contrary, he mounts the summit of the falls by a road cut through a vast hill of clay soil, extensive enough to supply brick clay for a large town. The tableau at the summit of the rock is quite unique. Standing, or, better still, lying on one's face, and peering over a rocky parapet one hundred feet above the basin, with the music of the "gorge" sounding sonorously to the left, a noble basin of water (which, from that height and distance, seems almost motionless, but which, toward the foot of the more distant falls, is full of dangerous and deceitful eddies) is beneath us. Its contour bends gracefully till it blends into the curving bank of the river, which seems like some vast silver snake in the brilliant sunlight; then further on, down through the trees, is seen a long and perfectly straight canal of Nature's construction, with walls of the deepest green foliage hemming it in from sunlight. The whole country parallel to the bank of the river seems as if it had been at one time under water, when the Muskoka River must have been a majestic and mighty torrent. Low plains, and shrubbery of birch and hazel clothe the right bank of the river below the High Falls, while the opposite side is covered to the water's edge with the "murmuring pines and the hemlocks."

But, taken all in all, perhaps the honors of monarchy must be given to the South Falls, when the rival attractions of these torrents are fairly weighed in the balance.

One specialty presented by the South Falls (about three miles from Bracebridge on the Gravenhurst Road) is that of unexpectedness. The traveller comes on the cataract unawares. He has not just mounted a steep hill, as in his last journey. He is driving along a comparatively level road, with nothing whatever to suggest cataracts, in the surrounding scenery, when suddenly he pulls up at the South Falls Bridge, and the raging scene of boiling waters almost takes away his breath. Deafened by their thunder, dazzled by their uprising spray, confused by the suddenness of the apparition, he gladly turns, to collect his thoughts, toward the upper portion of the river. He sees that this cataract differs from its rivals in having an upper as well as a lower basin, the soil on the left upper bank having been scooped out into a small lake, which boasts a little tree-clad island. Looking still higher up the river, he sees in the distance another waterfall which seems an incredibly tiny parent for the immense cataract behind him; and here, to calm the impatient statistician, we may say, in round numbers, that from the bridge to the lower basin is 1,000 feet, and that the descent is 100 feet. The writer had seen the falls from the bridge in the winter for an instant, but his first perfect inspection was in the summer. He accepted an invitation from C. W. Molesworth, C. E., to accompany him on his official visit of inspection to the government works then (and still) in progress at the falls, under the able direction of Mr. Gunn. The series of rocky waterfalls, however attractive to the searcher for the picturesque, has been a grievous drawback to the lumbermen, so much so that Mr. Boyd, who had intended operating largely in square timber, was forced to give up the project owing to the non-erection of a timber slide. The loss to the lumbermen is two-fold: first, the direct loss from the cruel bruising (often amounting to total destruction) which the logs receive in their descent to still water; secondly, and perhaps chiefly, the loss arising from delay, the logs having to run the gauntlet, while descending, of narrow gorges, one of which is (say) thirteen, and another seven feet wide. Hence jams are sure to ensue, and a tedious process of warping them out of the jams by windlasses, etc. (during which trees growing on the tops of the rocks come in very conveniently as *fulcra* to support the strain), becomes necessary, causing a delay which may last for weeks. The work now in progress, when completed,—as it is hoped, in time for next season's drive,—will give lumbermen a timber slide capable of delivering logs in safety, and at the rate of more than 600 per hour, to still water. The slide will be built along the left bank of the river, and will necessitate about 4,000 cubic yards of blasting. The blasting averages 18 feet depth of drilling per blast per day of ten hours. Mr. Molesworth is a veteran in the engineering profession, and, to dispel the idea that his office is a sinecure, it may be mentioned that on the day preceding that of this inspection he levelled over eleven miles of railway, then proceeded to Bracebridge, and on the 21st of August, 1878, travelled over three miles of the hilly and horribly "rutty" old road to Gravenhurst, made his inspection, and levelled over 1,100 feet, traversing rough and slippery crags, to slip from which would be instant death. On his return to Bracebridge he found a telegram summoning him back to Toronto by the first train. Such a rushing work would try the nerves of one twenty years younger than this veteran engineer of over eighteen years' standing in the Public Service.

A few more words on the scenic aspects of the South Falls: Below the bridge the water precipitates itself by two perpendicular leaps, followed by comparatively level basins, into a gradually contracting chasm, apparently eight feet, but really thirteen or fifteen feet wide. On the right bank a vast, almost perpendicular, smooth, dark, iron-colored rock is intersected by lighter colored seams, apparently mixtures of quartz and rosy feldspathic crystals. Near the angle where one of these seams intersects the water, and cutting the former at right angles, a new glory shone over the scene on the morning of the writer's visit—a veritable rainbow, partly across the foaming and comparatively level wedge of water at the base of the second fall in the series. The infinite variety of rainbow tints partly hid the sombre ledges which inclined transversely to the slope of the fall, and wreaths of rainbow seemed blown by the wind across the higher parts of the rock, trickling not only from spray but from infiltration of surface water through the strata. Out of reach of the cold damp portion of the rock, young maples and birches were flourishing in front of a screen of pines. Below the last of the series which comprise the South Falls, is a basin with a background of unbroken pine forest. The geological aspect of the left bank of the river is different: crags of what resemble grey sandstone appear in company with others, dazzling the eye by their micaseous glitter.

As the writer stood spell-bound by this glimpse of fairy land, amid so much stern and wrathful scenery, mentally photographing the rainbow, and, be it confessed, hopeless of descending lower over the confused labyrinth of crags and tangled undergrowth, the solitude was suddenly enlivened by the sight of a grave and venerable man, whose locks showed the whitening hand of Time. In fact, Mr. Sinclair, an old and respected resident of the South Falls village, was seen arising and hopping with goat-like agility from rock to rock. He, by his agile bounding, comforted the writer, who descended, and was pulled again up the face of a giant boulder by Mr. Sinclair, who showed him new points of view, till finally we reached the bottom of the cascade, and after a last upward glance at its snowing turmoil, we turned to inspect the floor of shingle, which consisted of water-worn stones from the size of an egg to that of a man's head, of all colors, and smooth, some being actually polished. This polishing was the laborious result of centuries of friction on the rocks, and some very remarkable round pockets or cups were seen worn in the rock by the perpetual rubbing of imprisoned pebbles.

It is a curious geological speculation to explain the share which the abrading action of damp and frost may have played in the formation of the chasm of the South Falls. It must have been very slight, or else have acted during inconceivably protracted cycles. There is nothing here, as in the Niagara rock, capable of being undermined or loosened, and little friable in the adamantine wall.

While dinner was in prospect, and Mr. Sinclair was carrying me off in triumph from other expectant hosts up a comparatively easy path to the village, and as we watched seven men armed with crowbars, up to their middles in the water above the bridge, wrestling with an isolated boulder stubbornly imbedded in the river bed, I thought of my visit to Niagara fifteen years ago, and could not help contrasting the social surroundings of the two scenes. Here all was quiet, no swearing, no drunkénness, but much unobtrusive courtesy. The villagers did not think necessary to gape at each tourist, or even at a journalist, as at a gratuitous peep-show. There was no guide with his monotonous droning repetition of guide-book platitudes, but on the contrary my cicerone indicated the point of view and then retired, knowing that we worship best before Nature's temple in silence. But think of Niagara with its greedy extortioners—the man who wants you to believe in and buy Niagara (Derbyshire) spar; and the second man who doesn't help you on with your oil-cloth suit and wants a dollar; and the third man who looks on at the second and wants a quarter; and the cabman, perched on an eminence like the queen of the Harpies, and gloating over the thought that he is charging you three times the lawful fare.

One addition, indeed, to the natural charms of all Muskoka scenery, is that quiet and freedom from pertinacious bores which it is possible for the tourist to enjoy. We have only given our readers a glimpse of the natural beauties of Muskoka. Let them fill in the details for themselves by personal inspection. They will return to the bricks and mortar of the city with renewed vigor of body and pleasant images of the glories of Nature, to be renewed in their memories during each annual Muskoka holiday.

Having now finished his address to the pleasure-seeking visitor, whose only object is to enjoy bracing air and beautiful scenery, and whom we might call the landscape tourist, let the writer next include

THE SPORTSMAN,

whether he be hunter, angler or trapper, among the list of his pupils. Sportsmen may be roughly divided into veterans and greenhorns. To the veterans he has little to say. It is not for him to teach a hunting or a fishing patriarch the mysteries of woodcraft or of angling. The tyro will learn more in the course of one day's journey under the guidance of our Bracebridge sporting Gamaliel, Mr. Wm. Higgins, than he could from the pages of a library devoted to minutiæ of the rod, field, and gun.

One item of advice he would *very strongly* press on all such intending visitors to Muskoka. Write to Mr. W. Higgins, if possible, at least a fortnight before starting. He is a veteran of about forty-five years' standing as a hunter and angler. He knows the bush, the lake, the river, the creek, and their dumb inhabitants, thoroughly.

During the course of a sporting lifetime, he has gathered up thousands of practical hints, those little things which make the difference between success and failure, about the ways and secret habits of the bear, the deer, and the pickerel. He has received honorable mention in this connection from the pen of Mr. Hallock, the author of the *Sportsman's Gazette*, an excellent and widely known sporting text book. He can also refer to Mr. Lauder, cattle breeder, Rochester, N. Y., and Dr. Paddock, New York. Tell Mr. Higgins what you are going to do, whether to fish or hunt, and how many will compose the party, and what guns, tents, or dogs you possess, also whether you are pressed for time; in short, make a clean breast to him of your aims and requirements. He will then advise you as to what to get in each particular case, and, if requested, can furnish whatever you may require better and cheaper than you can yourself in most cases. His general advice is to the following effect:

As to deer-hunting, the north-west part of Oakley is a good hunting ground, and tracks of moose are occasionally seen there. All round Trading Lake deer abound, and the deer-hunter need not undertake any very long or toilsome journey to find his favorite quarry. The shores of Muskoka Lake are a favorite haunt for deer. If a sportsman is pressed for time, he can often enjoy deer-hunting in the close vicinity of Bracebridge, and return to the village every night. If he has a good fox-hound (the best deer-hound is a cross between a bull dog and a blood-hound) or any deer-hound, let the dog come with him, and begin his training in company with experienced hounds. Mr. Higgins keeps from four to six deer-hounds on hand, and breeds hounds, so that there need be no failure of dogs, and if the sportsman feels so disposed, he need only bring his gun, which may be a Henry or Ballard rifle, though Mr. H. uses a Smith & Wesson. For one who is not in the habit of shooting with a rifle, a double-barrelled shot gun, guage Nos. 9 and 10 (for buckshot), is preferable. Sometimes the deer dashes through the open with such tremendous velocity that a tyro may miss him even at short range, whereas the wide-spreading of the buckshot will almost ensure the downfall of the antlered monarch. Plenty of canoes are to be hired in Bracebridge and its vicinity. Provisions and other camping requisites can be bought in Bracebridge cheaply, if not at or under Toronto prices. One party saved $15.00 by buying their outfit in Bracebridge.

As to fishing, Muskoka Lake is the *habitat* for black bass, pickerel, and salmon trout (trolling), while speckled trout are to be found of excellent quality in Trading Lake, twenty miles from Bracebridge. If the tourist prefers to buy his rods, artificial flies, etc., in Toronto, he can be recommended to Croft, Colborne Street. It is useless to advise Americans not to bring revolvers for deer-hunting, for they are sure to bring them naturally. Bears may be legally shot at any time, though the skin is most valuable in the fall. Bears have been very abundant this year (1878), and have come into the clearings, owing to the flooding of the swamps and scarcity of berries. Over forty bear skins were shipped by Mr. Beatty from Parry Sound.

The trapper can find mink, beaver, fisher, martin, and musk rat, not far from Bracebridge. An Indian recently made a handsome sum of money by trapping for mink, musk rat, and bank beaver, on the south branch, some four miles from Bracebridge, which village is the centre for all these fishing and hunting expeditions.

The writer has undertaken the tedious task of collecting and summarizing those portions of the official reports of surveys of townships which refer to fishing, and whence the following anglers and trappers' *vade mecum* is gathered:

" Muskoka Lake abounds with fish, salmon trout and bass being the most valuable. The Muskoka River, in Oakley, abounds with large speckled trout. Trading Lake abounds in fish; speckled trout of the first description are there caught in great abundance by the Indians; the woods abound in wolves, deer, otter, mink, martin, fisher and beaver. The Lake of Bays is a deep and clear lake, abounding with white fish, lake trout, and speckled trout. The lakes and streams in Humphrey abound with fish in variety, as salmon and speckled trout, white fish, pickerel, bass, perch, etc.; deer, rabbits and partridge are especially plentiful. The lakes all through Ferguson are of clear good water, and abound in all the varieties of fish usually found in the waters of Georgian Bay or Lake Huron. Ah-Mik and Se-Sebe Lakes (Chapman) abound with excellent fish, consisting of bass, pickerel, white fish, and speckled trout, the latter are frequently met with in some of the smaller streams; deer are quite plenty, numbers have been taken by the Indians, and latterly by other hunters; other game comparatively scarce. We met several signs of the moose deer —I saw one, a fine, noble looking animal. Round Lake (McMurrich) is well stocked with salmon trout, whereas bass, pickerel, etc., abound in Big Eye Lake, and in the Magnetewan speckled trout are also to be met with. Fish abound in Lake Nipissing and South River. In the former they consist of pike, bass, white fish, salmon, and sturgeon. South River and some of the smaller streams afford that beautiful fish, the speckled trout."

So much for the *ipsissima verba* of the surveyors. It may be added that in reply to the queries of the Select Standing Committee of the Dominion Parliament on Immigration and Colonization, twenty-three competent witnesses testified to the general abundance of brook and salmon trout, white fish, bass, pickerel, maskinonge,

pike, &c., in the electoral district of Muskoka, while Mr. Begg said (as to McMurrich), " Salmon trout, bass, white fish, herring, &c., are tolerably plentiful. Deer are to be found in the neighborhood, but are being rapidly exterminated by rapacious pot-hunters and wolves. Severe restrictions should be placed on the former, and a bounty offered for the scalps of the latter."

Mr. George Kelcey has kindly supplied the writer with the following items, with reference to Whitestone Lake and the Township of Hagerman :

" Around Whitestone Lake, before the country settled up, were the hunting grounds for the Indians, who killed large quantities of deer ; the deer made it (the neighborhood of the lake) their winter quarters. I went down the lake on the ice one morning, was away about 2½ hours, and counted 55 deer. They are not so thick now, but still there are great quantities which cross it on their way further north. Last winter (1877-'78), as near as I could calculate, by their fresh tracks across the lake, there must have been about 3000 which crossed my lot, which is the principal run-way for them. They don't stay round the lake now as they did formerly.

" The lakes abound with fish in this township. Whitestone, Shawanaga and Limestone Lake, contain pickerel, white fish, herring, suckers, catfish, &c. High Lake, Upper Lake and Lorrimer Lake, contain salmon trout and other fish, but not pickerel. Pickerel and trout are not found together. The fish are easily caught. The settlers take great quantities of pickerel about the middle of May, catching them with their hands at the foot of the rapids. I went to look on one night, taking a man and boy with me, who caught about 800 lbs. of pickerel in about 1½ hours. Quantities of herring are caught at the Narrows (the narrow channel connecting the two arms of Whitestone Lake), in the village of Dunchurch. In Nov.,'77, about 2200 lbs. were caught by one man in his nets in about 14 days. They are not quite so plentiful now. The herring sometimes will weigh as much as 2 lbs., the pickerel as high as 20 lbs. I caught eight myself that weighed 97 lbs."

The writer of this descriptive portion of the Atlas reached Hagerman too late in the autumn of 1874 for any fishing experiences. He saw evident signs of the presence of deer around Whitestone Lake. The marginal belt of underbrush showed evidence of having been cropped by the deer standing on the frozen surface of the lake during the previous winter. The bones of deer were also picked up, and these same bones, gnawed into sharp splinters by the field mice, were a grievous nuisance to barefooted boys or moccasined men.

During the winter an Indian camp was pitched at the opposite side of the road from the residence of Mr. G. Kelcey, where the writer then lived. Wading as best

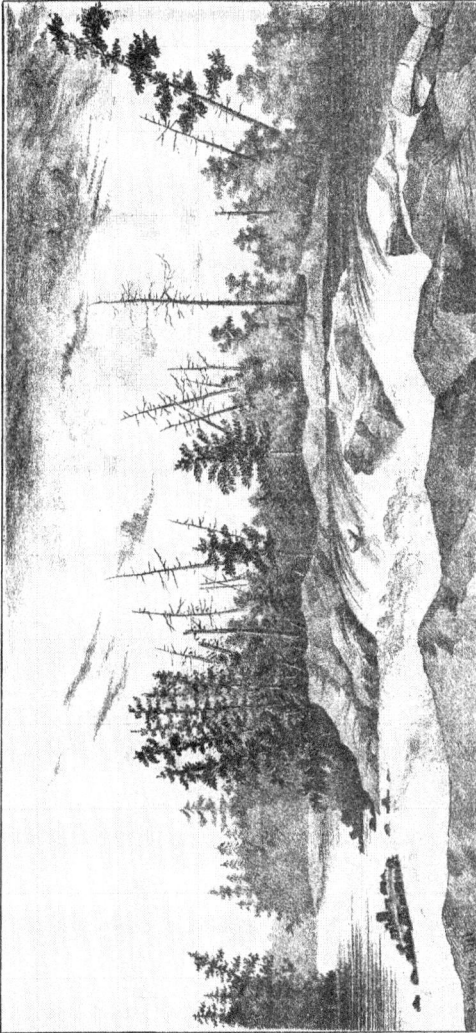

FALLS ON THE MUSQUASH RIVER, AT BALA.

he might through the deep snow, the writer followed his Indian guide, whose skill in woodcraft enabled him to find an instant clue to the labyrinth of trees, by certain small nicks made on the bark with a tomahawk, and so placed as to be visible each from its adjoining neighbors. Having reached the camp, a striking scene broke on the view. The Indian, with that exquisite instinct which seems his heritage, had pitched his tent in such a position with reference to a very large square boulder, that the camp was completely sheltered from the wind and cold. Between the boulder and the camp was a roaring fire; inside the camp a quiescent Indian in a dreamy state of repose, mentally wondering, perhaps, why christianity and scalping were opposed to each other, or whether the stories of the happy hunting grounds in paradise were not true after all. Deer-skins were hung on poles, the meat was being got ready for transport, dogs wandered round, sniffing in a contemptuous way at the deers' heads which cumbered the snow, and seemed inclined to nip our legs clandestinely, when we got out of the glare of the camp fire. Next day I saw an athletic young Indian yoked to a kind of harness, and dragging a large quantity of venison wrapped up in a deer-skin, which itself (with the hair so disposed as not to catch the snow) formed the vehicle of transport. During that winter of very deep snow ('74-'75), the deer herded together into what are called "yards," and were slaughtered in the most brutal and wanton fashion by men who shot or knocked them down with clubs. These savages had not even the excuse of being pot-hunters, for they, like the wolves, destroyed more than they could eat, and the deer in such a plight are too lean for food, while their skins are not then marketable. If the deer seriously injured the farmers' crops, one could understand this senseless butchery, but what conceivable object, other than the gratifying of wanton cruelty, could be attained by exterminating these beautiful and harmless animals (which in their season afford wholesome and delicious meat, and which by their presence attract large sums of money spent by tourist sportsmen), it is difficult to conceive. Many deer were also torn by stray dogs not strong enough to kill them outright, but able to lacerate and leave them to perish in lingering agony.

The following anecdotes from the *Free Grant Gazette* (published in Bracebridge), give a graphic picture of what the sportsman may enjoy in Muskoka. Taking up the files of the *Gazette*, at random, we light first on an episode (June, '77), not of deer-stalking or fishing, in the Township of Spence, but of a man-hunt:

"While two young men, sons of Mr. Croswell of the Township of Croft, were looking for their cows in the woods, on Monday the 4th inst., they saw a large bear some distance from them. A small dog which had accompanied them, on seeing bruin, immediately gave chase, but instead of making for the dog, the bear made for the young men. Seeing a cedar tree lodged in an ash tree, they both climbed the cedar and got into the ash tree. The bear followed them, and coming up to them, tore one of the boots off the eldest boy. The boy continued kicking; the young man succeeded in driving the bear down, but he very soon came back and made fresh attack. He tore the flesh from both sides of the bare foot, and put his tusks through the instep of the other boot in trying to drag the young man down the tree. The youngest boy broke a limb from the tree, and by using it on the bear succeeded in keeping him off, but the young men were kept in the tree from 8 a. m. to 2 p. m., when the bear left them. The wounded young man bound up his foot and made his way home, a distance of a mile and a half."

As a rule Muskoka bears, like their kindred elsewhere in Ontario, do not attack men, but the above incident, obtained from a thoroughly reliable source, shows that this rule has its exceptions, and points out the danger of rashly provoking bruin in his forest home.

Another "bear" item, from *F. G. G.*, McMurrich Township, August, '77:

"Mr. Duncan Morrison, agent for Cook Bros., was treed by a bear last week in this township, and the best of it is that there was a double treeing, for Morrison shouted to scare the bear, and the bear being scared ran up another tree."

Free Grant Gazette, August 17, 1877, Maganetawan:

"A settler here, named Johnson, while walking on a path through the bush, came suddenly upon a bear, which apparently was lying in wait. The bear jumped at Johnson, who fell backwards over a log. Bruin then bit his feet, and picked the man up, and after unmercifully squeezing him, commenced walking away with him; but at this period the cries of Johnson were heard by another man, who came in time to save him. The bear then climbed a tree."

F. G. G., August, '77, Ryerson:

"Very few deer to be seen this season. Pot-hunters last year, around Rainy Lake, killed large numbers, driving them into the lake wholesale with deer-hounds. A law should be passed to stop this wanton slaughter."

F. G. G., Oct. 5, '77, Brund:

"Deer are plentiful around Trading Lake; very little trapping; bears in abundance. Dr. Baddick and party, from New York, have just returned from Trading Lake, having had good sport. They killed thirteen deer, and eight wolves, of which they got four."

Port Sydney:

"The great hunters of the season in these parts are Mr. and Mrs. Stewart, and Mr. Murray, of this place, who on Thursday last chased, in their canoe, a moose. They ran it backwards and forwards for about four miles, vainly trying to kill it with small shot. Calling for assistance just as the animal was heading for Thoms' Bay, Mr. Thoms appeared, and, levelling his rifle, with one shot took the skin and Mrs. Stewart bore away triumphantly the head and immense branching horns—a trophy which the energetic huntress may well be proud of."

As a final bear item for 1877, it may be mentioned that on Dec. 5th, while Mr. J. A. Mackenzie (son of Mr. Mackenzie, C. E.,) and Mr. Pilch, of Perry, were out hunting, the dogs came on a den of bears under the roots of a large upturned pine. After a fierce fight, the dogs biting and the men firing in buckshot right between the bears' eyes, the she-bear charged fiercely, but finally the bears were all killed. The she-bear weighed 200 lbs., and the cubs 70 lbs. each. Here the dogs saved the lives of the hunters by keeping the bear at bay.

In the issue of the *F. G. G.*, Oct., 1878, we find the following from Port Sydney:

" Sporting is excellent here this season, deer having been killed in plenty—but Mrs. Stewart, the wife of Captain Stewart, of Mary Lake, has again become the heroine of the chase, eclipsing all the hunters in this vicinity. On Thursday last an immense moose swam across the lake and landed near Capt. Stewart's residence, their dog driving it back to the water. Capt. and Mrs. Stewart espied it, and whilst her husband was drawing small shot from his gun to load with buck-shot, the intrepid woman, accompanied by a young girl named Rose Hurbert, rushed to a canoe, and though there was a quantity of water in it, made chase after the animal for the purpose of keeping it in the lake until her husband, in a boat, should come to shoot it. Eager and exciting was the chase. They at length overtook it and succeeded in turning it in the direction of Thoms' Bay, where dwelt a sure shot, Mr. Thoms. Capt. Stewart soon came up with the moose and gave him a charge of buck-shot, which seemed to have no effect upon him. They then all shouted, and Mr. Thoms appeared in answer to the call—he seized his rifle and asked Capt. Stewart if he should shoot, as he did not wish to interfere with his sport. Capt. Stewart bade him fire, when there was at once a flash, a snort, a short struggle, and the noble animal lay dead upon the sun-bright waters. Mrs. Stewart will now have another trophy of her skill in the chase, in the shape of another pair of antlers to grace her residence, whilst Mr. Thoms will have a skin, which, when tanned, will make a splendid sofa cover, whereon he may recline when the hard farming work of a Muskoka day is over. This is the second moose that Mrs. Stewart has been principally instrumental in killing. May the favored huntress

surpass in skill and luck her great predecessor Diana. The animal weighed 700 lbs., and we have a grateful knowledge of the meat being wonderfully juicy and tender, but what is the best of venison without the sweet accessories? Not much!

JOHANNUS COMMUNICATUS."

We must now conclude this sporting section. Enough has been written to show what a field of enjoyment is found in Muskoka for the adventurous sportsman. The timid or the feeble need not venture too far into the bush without an escort. From the main bulk of sportsmen we have not tried to conceal that the excitement of occasional peril is not lacking, but when were men of Anglo-Saxon blood turned back from duty or from pleasure by the fear of human or bestial foes?

HISTORY.

The history of Muskoka (using this name to designate the two Free Grant territories) differs essentially from that of older settled counties in Canada. In many of the last named counties their history is continuously traceable from the first dawn of French dominion to the present hour, and is interwoven with the general history and historical biographies of Canada. This district, on the contrary, after coming incidentally into notice, in connection with the expedition of Champlain, seems to vanish from the ken of historians for more than two centuries, re-appearing, and beginning to assert its importance, towards the middle of the present century.

The pre-historic period of Muskoka life is full of the richest materials for romantic thought. We may picture the peaceful Huron, chased from his loved garden by the savage Iroquois. Swiftly he flies, but swifter is the pursuer—a foe whose warlike scowl never softened yet in pity; a few brief moments and the Huron writhes impaled, amid the jeers of his ruthless torturers, by the margin, it may be, of the Muskoka Lake, and breathing a dying prayer to the great, though dimly worshipped Manitou.

Indian relics, both mortuary and domestic, have been discovered in the adjoining County of Simcoe, and in Muskoka the evident traces of ancient Indian gardens are on record.

Proofs of former Indian occupation of this district are abundant on the south branch of the Muskoka River near the corner post which marks the junction of the Townships of Muskoka, Draper, Oakley and McLean, a thick second-growth covered the clearing formerly made by the Mohawk Indians. According to the statements of an old Indian Chief, deceased some six years ago, these Mohawk pioneers of Muskoka settlement were driven away and dispersed after a succession of sanguinary engagements by another tribe of Indians who hunted and fished near Trading Lake. In Macaulay a piece of land some thirty-five acres in extent, and perfectly clear from rock or stump, was also discovered by one of the early settlers, and was the result of Indian toil. Again, in clearing the Alport farm near Bracebridge, arrow heads, tomahawks, and the remains of a stone fire-place were discovered, the former being of evident Indian origin, and the fire-place being, on the contrary, a relic of by-gone white adventurers. From the size of the trees the relics thus unearthed beneath their roots must have been at least a century old.

The little that Canadian history proper tells us of Muskoka may be briefly glanced at. In 1615-16, in the narrative of Champlain's expedition, we find the following quoted in "Tuttle's Illustrated History of the Dominion of Canada": "Always desirous to embark in any enterprise which promised to make him better acquainted with the country, Champlain laid down a plan of operations which he offered to aid the Algonquins in carrying out, and at which they expressed the utmost satisfaction. He accompanied them in a long march, first up the Ottawa, and afterwards over small lakes and portages, leading to Lake Nipissing. The Nipissings, about 700 or 800 in number, who inhabited the shores of this lake, received the party in a friendly manner. Having remained with them for two days, the Algonquins resumed their journey along the course of French River to Georgian Bay, which they crossed near the Great Manitoulin Island, and entered Lake Huron, which Champlain describes in his travels as a fresh-water sea 200 leagues in length by 50 in breadth." In 1639, the Hurons numbered over twenty thousand souls, according to the Jesuit census. They built villages, had much mechanical skill, and seemed fitted for becoming ultimately a civilized and industrious nation. For the conversion of the Hurons, the Jesuits labored assiduously, traversing the route from the Ottawa to Lake Nipissing. "For fifteen years [Withrow's History of Canada] the missionaries toiled among the Hurons, in the country between Lake Simcoe and the Georgian Bay, at first with little effect, but finally with great success. Footsore and weary, gnawed by hunger and chilled by piercing cold, they traversed the wintry woods from plague-smitten town to town, to minister their healing simples to the victims of the loathsome small pox; to baptize, if possible, a dying child, and to tell the painted savages in their reeking wigwams of the love of Mary and her Divine Son." It may be added that an unbroken succession of Jesuit missions has been kept up since these early times to the Georgian Bay, and to the Severn River, which Father Proulx ascended about 1840. The Manitoulin Mission was organized

about the beginning of the present century, and included the east shore of the Georgian Bay, and of Lake Nipissing and French River.

To return to the Indians. The Hurons were finally almost exterminated by the Iroquois, and another interesting and peculiar Indian race, the Nipissings, living by the lake of the same name, were also driven away by the Iroquois, and forced to abandon their peaceful traffic in dried fish and furs. They were a branch of the Algonquins, and retained a peculiar custom of feasts for dead, being deemed sorcerers by the French. They had received Jesuit missionaries at points along the shores of Lake Nipissing, and after their flight from that region they joined the Iroquois and Algonquin mission at the Lake of the Two Mountains, where a remnant still exists. Before dismissing the subject of the aboriginal settlers, we remark that the Indians have left their impress on the topographical vocabulary of the Muskoka district. These names, always mellifluous and suggestive, are happily to some extent retained amongst us. Thus Muskoka is now widely known to the reading public of Great Britain, through the medium of a tale published in *All the Year Round*, and the name is there stated to mean "clear sky land." This is an erroneous derivation. True it is that the name of an Indian doctor or conjurer, who lived in Muskoka, might be so translated, but Muskoka takes its name from a greater celebrity, even the warrior "Mesqua Ukee" (not easily turned back in the day of battle.) He fought side by side with the British in the war of 1812, and received the much coveted medal, bearing the image of King George on its silver surface. Mesqua Ukee was head chief of the Rama Indians, and lived in Rama. What is now called Muskoka, was then divided into Indian hunting grounds, and the south branch of the Muskoka River was the exclusive patrimony of Mesqua Ukee. True it is that Begamagobaway (who lived in Port Carling, and whose heir is now chief of the Parry Sound Indians) ruled over a small section of the Hurons (or Objibeways), which section we might call the Muskoka Indians; but he was as the twinkling of a small star before the moon, when compared with Mesqua Ukee. Not only the south branch of the Muskoka River, but even the lake itself, and ultimately the whole district, became called after the great Chief Mesqua Ukee. It will be easily seen how a slight corruption of the name gave us Muskoka, instead of Mesqua Ukee. As Amerigo filched the honor of sponsorship of this continent from Columbus, so the crafty conqueror Misquedoh (clear sky) has been chronicled as the god-father of Muskoka in place of the undaunted Mesqua Ukee.

Passing over the long protracted labors of Captain Bayfield, in surveying the Georgian Bay, and without pausing to chronicle the doings of the Hudson Bay, and other hunters and trappers, let us now plunge into the brief and modern history of Muskoka.

In 1858 the government commenced the building of a road from Washago to the interior of Muskoka, a road which, necessarily piercing rocky fastnesses of forbidding aspect, disheartened many a weary traveller who jolted over its cavities and excrescences with aching bones, instead of viewing the rocks with half-closed eyes from the soft medium of a railroad couch. In the latter part of 1859 the road had been opened to South Falls, and the bridge was not then built. In fact the two branches of the Muskoka River formed two formidable bars to any emigrant invasion of this territory. Bracebridge did not then exist, even on paper, and an amusing circumstance is still remembered of a settler, at a somewhat later period, trying to cross the Muskoka River on a pine tree near where our Bracebridge bridge now spans it. The settler had been imbibing liberally, and his devious course over the log upset the centre of gravity. He would have made food for pickerel, and a neat illustration for temperance lecturers, but his ruin, in the shape of a demijohn which he carried with him, proved his salvation, since it being tied to him hung on one side of the tree and balanced him, while he hung on the other, and was thus saved.

Before it was finally decided to open up Muskoka and Parry Sound by a free grant colonization road, itself the forerunner of the bold and successful experiment of general free grants, the idea was seriously mooted in high quarters of throwing the whole district into one vast Indian reservation.

This scheme, however, fell to the ground, and in 1859, Mr. R. J. Oliver was appointed locating agent, met the settlers in October of the same year at Severn Bridge, and issued seventeen location tickets of land adjoining the road. In 1861 Morrison, Muskoka, Draper, and Macaulay were offered for location.

At this time settlers lived a very isolated life, far from each other, and far not merely from the great centres of civilization, but from those lesser centres which furnished them with the necessaries of life. Some had to walk forty miles to Orillia to buy provisions or to mail a letter. They had to carry their flour home on their backs over so-called "roads" of the most wretched description. On one occasion settlers from the Townships of Muskoka and Draper, finding no flour in Orillia, had to walk a distance of sixty miles to Barrie, and "back" the flour home. So isolated was the life of many a settler in the bush, that they almost lost count of times and seasons, and one man was thus encountered who had been keeping Tuesday as the Lord's day for many months.

In 1861 Mr. R. J. Oliver crossed the north branch of the Muskoka River on the pine log above referred to, and met John Beal and David Smith, who were the first settlers north of the Falls. In the same year Mr. Thomas McMurray had only one neighbor within many miles of him, was twenty-one miles from the nearest Post Office, and thirty-five from the nearest grist mill. There was only one settler in Draper, Macaulay, Stephenson, McLean, Brunel, Ryde, Oakley, Chaffey, Monck, Watt, Humphrey, Wood, and Medora. There was one house on the river, where Mr. A. Bailey and family resided.

It is with somewhat of the relish with which a storm-tossed sailor, in the cosy sitting room of his hotel, recounts the recent fury of the ocean, that settlers, now comfortable, rehearse the former trials which tested their endurance, while reminiscences of meals on birch buds, and of seed-potatoes dug up for food through grim necessity, give zest to the enjoyment of plenteous viands. Things gradually mended, and the once solitary settler encountered, in amazement, new neighbors in his rambles through the bush. Families clustered together, school-houses, often built on land given by the settlers, appeared. The faithful missionary held occasional, and then more regular services, in the fast-increasing centres of population. New townships were surveyed, and others organized, with all the paraphrenalia of Reeves and Councils. Settlers from the British isles, of good standing at home, and possessed of means, began to buy improved farms, and thus ready money—that one thing needful to cap the social pyramid—began to circulate more freely. This progress has been continuous up to the present hour, but the rate of increase has itself increased with great rapidity. Since the appointment (in May) of the present immigration agent at Bracebridge (who is also the writer of this history), *at least* $28,000 of immigrant capital (exclusive of value of personal effects) has entered Muskoka from the Toronto agency, and through the indefatigable exertions of Mr. John A. Donaldson, the Dominion Agent in that city. Valuable settlers have also reached Muskoka from the Hamilton agency of the Dominion Government, ably presided over by Mr. Smith, Mr. Donaldson's *confrere*. Mr. Donaldson may congratulate himself on the result of his exertions, which have resulted in the augmentation of our population by some very valuable settlers, who have no reason to regret their choice of new homes in the District of Muskoka. Through the Bracebridge Agency, immigrants are distributed to the Townships of Macaulay, McLean, Ridout, and others in the Bracebridge Crown Lands Agency, besides those further north, and also occasionally to Parry Sound in winter, and to the Swiss settlement, which has been inaugurated under the auspices of Baroness Von Koerber, in the Maganetawan district. The total number of immigrants entered on the books of the Bracebridge Agency from May to December, 1879, inclusive, has been

123, but a few who possess more or less means do not report themselves to the agent. In 1872, the first election was held for representative in the Commons. The leading event of 1874 was the visit of Lord Dufferin, Governor-General of Canada, to Bracebridge and other parts of Muskoka and Parry Sound. Had the most insignificant and unintelligent commoner then occupied the vice-regal throne, he would have been received with respect as the delegate of the Queen to her Muskoka people. But when we remember the then Viceroy was of high rank and social standing, a gifted author, and a most admirable public speaker, that the hereditary legacy of genius descended from Sheridan had not been buried in darkness, but cultivated laboriously by him, and when we also remember that this was the pioneer visit of a Viceroy to Muskoka, we may easily realize the enthusiasm which followed his footsteps as he journeyed, and made his progress a sequence of sincere ovations.

He visited Bracebridge on the 27th of July. The din of workmen's hammers had hardly ceased as they put the finishing strokes to the eight arches which spanned the village streets, when, at 7 o'clock p. m., the steamer "Nipissing," with His Excellency, the Countess, and suite on board, was seen coming alongside the Bracebridge wharf. They drove round the principal streets of the village, and finally reached the platform, where an excellently framed address was presented to His Excellency, and rewarded by a suitable reply. Lord Dufferin, after leaving Bracebridge, proceeded by steamer to Port Cockburn, and thence by land to Parry Sound, where he bid farewell to the Free Grant Districts, his progress being one continued triumph. He stopped at the settlers' homes, conversed with them, and specially interested himself in an Icelandic settler. No doubt a future edition of the Atlas will chronicle a similar visit of his successor, the Marquis of Lorne.

1876.—A resolution was passed in the Local House (Feb. 4th), offering a bonus of $8,000 per mile for the construction of an extension of the Northern Railway to connect with the Georgian Bay Branch of the Canada Pacific Railway near Lake Nipissing.

A radical change was made by an Act passed in the Local House in the regulation of licenses for the sale of liquor. The inspection and licensing of Taverns was taken out of the hands of Municipal Councils and transferred to inspectors appointed by the Local Government. The present efficient inspector, Mr. E. F. Stephenson, who was the first appointed under the new system for the district of Muskoka, is of opinion that the present system has worked admirably, and the result has been less illicit vending of liquors and more orderly conduct of hotels than formerly existed. There are some thirty licensed houses in the license district of Muskoka.

In October, 1876, vigorous efforts were made to induce the Government to put the road from Bracebridge to Huntsville in thorough repair. This artery of travel accommodates the traffic of nine townships of Muskoka proper, and about twelve of Parry Sound, while it is fed by nine important tributary roads which pierce large settlements.

1877.—The Attorney-General introduced an amendatory Act, of which the provisions, so far as they relate to Muskoka, may be thus summarized:

1. The Lieut.-Governor may direct the Commissioners of Public Works to erect lock-ups or jails.

2. Such lock-ups or jails to be common jails for prisoners sentenced for thirty days or less, pending removal to Barrie. The magistrate may still send them direct to Barrie.

3. The Parry Sound or Bracebridge stipendiary magistrate may interchange Division Court duties by mutual consent with the junior judge of Simcoe.

4. Any municipality of Muskoka not already in the judicial district of Simcoe is thereto annexed without extending the jury law of Ontario to such a municipality.

The fourth provision was an excellent step towards removing anomalies in the government of Muskoka. The Hon. Mr. Pardee introduced an Act for the quieting of doubts relative to the conjoint working of lumber licenses and the Free Grant Act. The Act deals with the case of a timber license overlapping the patent, where the locatee on a free grant has got his patent, and therefore has received a conveyance in fee simple of the pine trees existing or remaining on his land before the expiry of the timber license in force over his land. This Act declares substantially that the lumberman cannot be interfered with as to cutting the pine until the time of his license has expired. As there are annual licenses, the maximum overlapping being twelve months, a period which could only be reached by an unlikely chapter of accidents, but in any case the rights of the patentee are only held in abeyance for the time of the unexpired portion of the license. He enjoys all the equities, and can (with this restriction) convey, alienate, mortgage, or sell his farm immediately on receipt of the patent, except that, unlike real estate in other portions of the Province, his wife must not only bar her dower, but join in the deed as a grantee.

In the same year Mr. J. C. Miller, M. P. P., introduced an act (unfortunately but necessarily withdrawn, owing to its cold reception by the House) to enable the settler to do systematically and of right what he can do at present through the favor of the Crown Lands Department, namely, to sell his improvements, placing the buyer precisely in his thus relinquished position on the books of the Crown Lands office, as to remaining settlement duties.

(For these duties see Appendix A.) An excellent feature in this proposed amendatory Act was the permission sought to be given to the vendor to re-locate, and begin Free Grant life anew. There are many adventurous men loving the solitude of the forest who make admirable pioneers, and to whom " pulling up stakes" and breaking fresh ground in the wilderness is only a commonplace event. Mr. Miller's Act sought to enable such men to get a little cash together by selling their improvements, and with this fresh start to make a fresh opening in the forest. A wave of small capitalists would have thus followed the original wave of pioneers and the speed of settlement would have been greatly quickened. The settler can practically do this, but not as of right, and he cannot re-locate. The department, so to speak, washes its hand of him, and tells him that having sold his inheritance he is an alien from Free Grant privileges.

The Bishop of Algoma arrived in February, and made an extended missionary tour through Muskoka and Parry Sound.

The first consignment of oats and wheat ever received from Ryerson Township arrived at Bracebridge.

The first instalment of sixty farmers, some of whom were wealthy, and all from Haldimand County, passed through Bracebridge in March *en route* for Ryerson Township.

A great boon was granted to those living at a distance from Bracebridge, and who had formerly to travel long distances to attend the Division Court in that village, three additional Division Courts having been established in Severn Bridge, Huntsville, and Port Carling.

Gold was discovered in Gravenhurst in April, and a small imbedded nugget from the diggings being analyzed in Bracebridge, was found to be gold of considerable purity.

A large party of Swiss immigrants passed through Rosseau in July, *en route* for the Maganetawan, and under the superintendence of Baroness von Koerber.

In October a very heavy rush of settlers set in, the wharfinger at Bracebridge having to wait up at night discharging trunks, &c., and the hotels at Huntsville being so full that the new arrivals had to sleep as best they could on floors and tables. The settlers came from Stratford, Garafraxa, Chatham, and various parts of Western Ontario. Forty thousand acres were located through the Bracebridge Crown Lands Office alone.

The agitation for the erection of Muskoka proper (with possibly a slight rectification of its frontier), into a provisional county, was the most important event of this year. Very energetic efforts were made, both through the columns of the *Free Grant Gazette*, and by private canvass, to mould public opinion favorably towards this great and desirable change. It was defeated mainly

through the timidity and want of foresight of those who resist change simply because it *is* change. Nothing can long delay the erection of Muskoka into a county, but if this provisional county scheme had been carried, we should have gained the benefit of an apprenticeship, so to speak, under the provisional system, before being launched into full county organization. At that time, also, the Ontario Government would have carried the measure through without cost to the district, so that the opponents of the measure gained a very barren victory, prolonging the present state of county confusion under which Muskoka suffers, and denying us an inexpensive and gradual transition into the new county system. The phrase "county confusion," used in the last sentence, may seem a strange one, but it is expressive of our present system. Muskoka is portioned for county purposes between the Counties of Simcoe and Victoria, while the Parry Sound District is in certain respects a "no man's land," so far as county representation is concerned. The evils of the system are widely ramified, extending to the minutiæ of our municipal and educational affairs. There is one school inspector for Macaulay (in the county Victoria), and another for the adjoining Township of Monck, which is in Simcoe. The Parry Sound schools are inspected by a third inspector from Collingwood. If it is needful to make a road between Macaulay and Monck, application must first be made to the County Council at Lindsay. Then, if the request be granted, nothing can be done till the Simcoe Council sits, and a correspondence must take place between the two counties.

Again, suppose that the taxes remain unpaid on a lot in Bracebridge, valuable for position but unimproved, after the limit of time allowed by law, the lot is sold in Lindsay. Parties in Bracebridge who know its value know nothing about the sale, and cannot attend it. The competitors in Lindsay only know of it as an unimproved lot, and it is perhaps sacrificed to some speculator who may lock it up for years from improvement, whereas if we had a county, the sales would be at Bracebridge, and citizens of the village would buy such lots and build on them. This is a minor example, but the sum total of the various minor evils of our double municipal representation (in Lindsay and in Barrie), make a formidable aggregate, in addition to the more prominent disadvantage of loss of prestige and the impossibility of our Muskoka Reeves taking any concerted action on the joint interests of their constituents.

Towards the close of the year an excellent educational step in advance was taken by the formation, under the auspices of Mr. McGill (public school teacher in Bracebridge), ably encouraged by the Inspector for North Victoria, Mr. H. Reazin, viz., the formation of a Teachers' Association for Muskoka, to meet half-yearly in Bracebridge.

In 1877 a very vigorous step was taken in the direction of manufacturing progress, by the Bracebridge Council. They submitted a by-law to the people for the purpose of granting a bonus to the firm of Beardmore Bros., of Toronto, of $2000 (with exemption from taxation for ten years, of the proposed site of tannery to be erected by that firm). The all but unanimous passing of the by-law was speedily followed by the erection of the tannery, which has since been enlarged, and carried out on a much larger scale than that contemplated in the by-law, which only bound the firm to employ twelve instead of their present staff of 30 men. The magnitude of the scale on which the Beardmore tannery is conducted, and the fact that the purchase money for bark finds its way to fertilize the purses of settlers, within a radius of fifteen miles from Bracebridge, justify the insertion of a reference to this industry in the general history of Muskoka, though the whole burden of the bonus and other expenses has been borne by the village of Bracebridge.

This year was very largely devoted in Muskoka, as elsewhere, to political excitement. After a hard contest, during which he bore testimony to the honorable conduct of Mr. W. E. O'Brien, his opponent, Mr. A. P. Cockburn was again returned to represent these Free Grant districts in the Dominion Parliament.

Two semi-annual meetings of the teachers of Muskoka were held in Bracebridge in June and December, respectively. They were very successful, and reflected great credit on the Bracebridge school teacher, Mr. McGill (who is a scholar of Toronto University), who originated the convention. At the June convention, the teachers were favored with the presence of Mr. Reazin, Inspector for North Victoria, and also of the Honorable Adam Crooks, Minister of Education for the Province of Ontario, who delivered an exhaustive and masterly address on the educational system of this Province, in the Dufferin Hall. The year 1878 was marked by considerable activity in building operations, which in the village of Gravenhurst alone amounted, it is believed, to over $17,000.

The records of newspaper enterprise in Muskoka may be grouped together at the close of these annals. Keenly critical readers create vigorous journalism, and such are the people of Muskoka, ever on the alert to unearth the slightest typographical error, or false date; nor is there any dearth of crisp and incisive correspondence. Having such materials to work with, even at that early period, the *Northern Advocate*, the pioneer journal of the district, was started by Mr. Thos. McMurray. It was transferred to Bracebridge (Sept., 1870) and ably conducted under the editorial charge of Mr. James Boyer, our present village clerk. Much valuable information as to Muskoka and its

resources was then circulated amongst intending immigrants and settlers, both in Canada and Great Britain. After Mr. McMurray's failure in 1874, it was bought by Mr. Courtney, continued in Bracebridge, and abandoned after the death by drowning of the latter gentleman. Meanwhile the publication of the *Free Grant Gazette* was commenced by Mr. E. F. Stephenson, the present proprietor, in 1871, and continues now under the same ownership. The publication of the *Gazette* led to a large reduction in the price of newspaper work and job work. Mr. Stephenson also carried on the publication of the Huntsville *Liberal*, under the editorship of Mr. Howland. After the discontinuance of the *Liberal*, the Huntsville *Forester* made its appearance on Nov. 2nd, 1877, and is still published in that village.

On May 19th, 1876, Gravenhurst felt the journalistic wave, and saw the first number of *The Lumberman*, a publication which lived till Nov. 24th of the same year. Mr. E. F. Stephenson also, for a time, established a job office at Gravenhurst.

Meanwhile Mr. McMurray, the former proprietor of the *Advocate*, who is now Crown Lands Agent at Parry Sound, commenced in 1874, and still continues, the publication of the *North Star* in that village.

In April, 1878, the village of Bracebridge saw the advent of the *Herald*, a Conservative journal (Messrs. Graffe & Co., proprietors), which is still continued—the *Free Grant Gazette* being the organ of the Reformers. All the journals which have been chronicled are weekly newspapers devoted to the presentation of general and local news, and the present list consists of the *Free Grant Gazette* and *Herald* (both published in Bracebridge), the *Forester*, issued in Huntsville, and the *North Star* in Parry Sound.

A non-political glance at the parliamentary history of the district may be lastly given.

Muskoka has now double representation, namely, in Ottawa and Toronto. In 1867 the constituency—that is, the then existing nucleus of Muskoka, namely, the new Townships of Morrison and Macaulay—formed part of North Victoria. Mr. A. P. Cockburn was elected for the Local House to represent it, having defeated the late Joseph Staples by a majority of 269. In 1875 the first election for a representative in the Local House occurred, and Mr. J. C. Miller, our present member, was the successful candidate, his opponent being the late Mr. Long, of Bracebridge. A petition against his return was tried by the Judge in the Dufferin Hall, Bracebridge, and adversely to Mr. Miller. The decision was reversed, however, by the full Bench.

Mr. A. P. Cockburn (Reform) was the first Dominion representative of Muskoka, having defeated the late Mr. D'Arcy Boulton by a majority of 126. Again, in 1874, he was elected to the Dominion Parliament by a majority of 309 over the late Mr. Teviotdale of Bracebridge. At the last general election in 1878, Mr. Cockburn was again returned to represent Muskoka in the Ottawa Parliament, by a majority of 74 over Mr. W. E. O'Brien, of Shanty Bay, County Simcoe.

In bringing the history to a close, let the writer disclaim any intention of presenting it to the public as either exhaustive or perfect. It is only a bird's-eye view of some of the leading incidents in the progress of Muskoka, from zero to its present flourishing condition. More minute details, however, will be found elsewhere in the description of localities and townships.

NAVIGATION.

The progress of navigation in Muskoka is so important, and so excellent an index of the general progress of the settlement, that it is here treated as a separate sub-head, instead of being scattered through the general body of the history. It is substantially that given in the "Undeveloped Portions of Ontario," but revised up to the close of navigation in 1878. Many requisites for successful steam navigation in the inland waters of Muskoka—early opening and late closing of the lakes and rivers, depth of waters, rapid deepening of the waters as we recede from the shore, excellence of harbors, freedom from incrustation of boilers, but above all the long and convenient water stretches placed by Nature just where they can be utilized for the highways of colonization. During a great part of the year we are thus, in many localities, independent of roads, and we have a sure and cheap mode of transporting heavy freight, and also ready-made highways for the moving of lumber. All these advantages, however, would have been barren, had not some one been found of sufficient foresight to realize the future importance of Muskoka, and sufficiently enterprising to risk his means in developing that future, and of enjoying that influence with the Government which would constrain them to do their part in rendering the enterprise possible. Such a man was Mr. A. P. Cockburn, our present Dominion representative. In these days of our prosperity, when the districts are intersected by a net-work of roads, telegraphs, steam navigation, stage lines, and post offices, and when so many energetic speculators are ready to put a steamer on any lake or river where the least chance of traffic exists, the establishment of a new steamboat line is taken as a matter of course, and the addition of a new steamer on an old route hardly excites comment. It is with difficulty, therefore, that we retrace the stream of Time, and, in imagination, live under the disadvantages and gloomy prospects which might well have appalled Mr. Cockburn in his efforts to initiate steam navigation in Muskoka in 1865.

Let us then briefly trace the history of Muskoka navigation, remembering that even now the bulk of the traffic, whether immigrant or commercial, of Muskoka, and of those portions of Parry Sound which are tributary to Rousseau and Bracebridge, is carried over the lakes Muskoka, Rousseau and Joseph, and also the Muskoka River, so that the history of our navigation is the history of our progress, the overflowing freight houses and increasing fleet of steamboats refute the sneers of the enemies of Muskoka with dumb but unanswerable power. The first human ripple on the surface of these waters proceeded from the bark canoe of the untutored red man. In the same frail craft, doubtless, John Bell reached the Township of Macaulay in 1861. He is said to have spent five days in discovering the mouth of the river in order to reach the North Falls (now the flourishing village of Bracebridge). Mr. James Cooper introduced the first wood-boat in 1862, to be followed by McCabe's sail-boat in 1863, and Mr. James Sharpe's in 1864. All three boats were employed in the business of carrying passengers and freight to various points on the lakes. The rates then charged for land and water transportation were 75cts. per cwt. between Washago (the head of Lake Simcoe route) and Gravenhurst, or $1 per cwt. all land carriage. Mr. Holditch, about this time, constructed a large flat-boat to be propelled by horse-power. The boat was built at the North Falls (Bracebridge), and made a trip to McCabe's Bay (Gravenhurst), but never returned again, the craft, or rather its propelling arrangements, being a failure. The boat occupied upwards of twelve hours going on her trip (now performed in less than two hours). About the same time the Bradley Bros. built an expensive sloop for the trade, but it, like the horse-boat, was a failure.

In September, 1865, Mr. A. P. Cockburn, now representing Muskoka and Parry Sound in the Dominion Parliament, but then merchant and Reeve of the Township of Eldon, in the County of Victoria, made an examination of the Muskoka region, including the Lake of Bays, Peninsula, Vernon, and Fairy Lakes, and the Maganetawan River, returning by way of Lake Muskoka, and he was much impressed with the beauty and importance of these lakes. He returned shortly afterwards in company with Mr. James Cooper, sailed over Lake Muskoka to examine the reputed natural obstructions to navigation at Indian Village, now Port Carling. Mr. Cockburn then forwarded a paper on the back country to Hon. T. D. McGee, the then Commissioner of Agriculture, with a report of his observations, and some practical suggestions of a policy of road and other improvements which, if the Government would promise to make, he would undertake to place a steamer on the lakes to facilitate settlement. Mr. McGee and the Government felt highly

STEAMER "NIPISSING"

RUNNING DAILY BETWEEN GRAVENHURST, BRACEBRIDGE, PORT CARLING, AND
ROSSEAU. AND TRI-WEEKLY TO PORT COCKBURN, LAKE JOSEPH

pleased and interested in Mr. Cockburn's representations; and, in particular, Mr. McGee returned Mr. Cockburn's communication with a flattering request that Mr. C. should have it printed, which was done under the title of "A Few Weeks in the North." The result of these negotiations was that the keel of the "Wenonah" was immediately laid, and the steamer opened up steam navigation trade by making her first trip in 1866, arriving at North Falls (Bracebridge) when there was not twenty people in the place to greet her arrival. The rate of freight from Washago to North Falls was reduced at once from 75cts and $1.00 per cwt. down to 40cts. per cwt., and freight was always brought through punctually from McCabe's Bay (Gravenhurst). The "Wenonah" continued to ply alone, and generally at a loss to its owner, until in 1869 the "Waubamik" was brought up to assist in the dispatch of the growing traffic. In 1871 the fine low pressure steamer "Nipissing" was added, and in the spring of 1876 the powerful steam tug "Simcoe" formed another auxiliary in the Muskoka fleet. In 1877 a marine slip (or railway) was constructed at Gravenhurst, on which the "Nipissing" was raised, overhauled and a hurricane deck added, together with a cabin on the promenade deck. A large scow was also built, which has been utilized for the conveyance of lime, tan-bark, etc.

The steamer "Northern" was launched at Port Sydney in 1877, and plies between that village, Huntsville, and other ports on Mary, Fairy and Vernon Lakes.

In 1878, the "Dean" was transported by land carriage from Gravenhurst to Trading Lake, and plies between Baysville and a number of ports on Trading Lake and Lake of Bays.

A small steam launch, owned by Messrs. Rodick and Rogers, plies on Muskoka, Rosseau and Joseph Lakes for the service of tourists in the season.

There is also a steamer running on the Maganetawan River and Se-Sebe Lake as far as Burke's Falls, about thirty miles steaming altogether.

The latest addition to the steamer fleet of Muskoka and Parry Sound is a steamer belonging to Messrs. Charlebois and Flood, the contractors for the Georgian Bay Branch, and plying between the mouth of French River and the terminus of the road.

DESCRIPTION OF TOWNSHIPS.

MUSKOKA AGENCY.

In the Muskoka Agency there are eighteen townships now open for location as free grants, viz :—Brunel, Chaffey, Draper, Franklin, Macaulay, Medora, Monck, Morrison, Muskoka, McLean, Oakley, Ridout, Ryde, Stephenson, Slisted, Watt, Wood and Cardwell. The last named township, although in the Muskoka District, is attached to the Parry Sound Agency, and persons wishing to locate in that township must apply to the agent at Parry Sound. The Crown Land Agent at Bracebridge for the above townships is Mr. Aubrey White.

MORRISON.

The Township of Morrison was surveyed in 1860 by Mr. J. O'Brien, P.L.S. It contains 41,633 acres of land. It is the most southerly township in the Muskoka District, and is divided from the County of Simcoe by the Severn River. About one-half the township is settled, the district round Sparrow Lake containing some fine farms. The district west of the Muskoka Road is, however, with the exception a strip along the south boundary and a small portion near Lake Kab-she-she-bog-a-mog, totally unfit for settlement.

The village of Severn Bridge, at the crossing of the Severn River, contains two stores, hotel, post office, telegraph office, Orange Hall, and other buildings. There is also another hotel at the station of the Northern Railway across the bridge.

The Northern Railway traverses this township from south to north, and has one station—Lethbridge—about half way between Severn Bridge and Gravenhurst.

MUSKOKA.

This township contains 33,777 acres, of which 9000 appeared to be unlocated last year. It contains abundant water-power for mill or other machinery. The official surveys state that the best part of the township is in the north-east part, bordering on the Muskoka River on both its branches, along the Hock Rock River (the only stream except Muskoka River of any importance in the township), and around the head of Muskoka Bay. The islands are generally timbered masses of rock. The fish caught in the waters of the township are pickerel and bass in the summer, and white fish and trout in the fall.

GRAVENHURST, the present Muskoka terminus of the Northern Railway, lies in the township, and contains (Dec., 1878) about 200 houses, one hardware store, eight dry goods stores, eleven shingle mills, two shoemakers, one tailor, two watchmakers, three dressmakers, two saddlers, one attorney-at-law, four hotels, two bakers, one butcher, one book store, one flour and feed store, one doctor, one drug store, one foundry, boarding house, three telegraph offices, express office, Gravenhurst and Muskoka wharf, railway stations with waiting rooms, ticket offices, freight sheds, wind mill, pumps, etc. It possesses a Town Hall (with lock-up underneath), public school and four churches, and claims 1,200 inhabitants. Some idea of the importance of Gravenhurst as a distributing station on the Northern may be gathered from the fact that 2811 tons 1210 lbs. of freight (much of it of a most costly nature), left the railway freight house in 1878 for various parts of Muskoka. Nature has given to each of our incorporated villages special advantages. Parry Sound has its unrivalled harbor, from which a vessel could make the voyage to Liverpool. Bracebridge is the end of navigation on the Muskoka River. Gravenhurst is the distributing and manufacturing point for an immense quantity of the products of Muskoka forests.

RYDE.

It contains 39,500 acres of land, and 928 of water, many excellent hard wood valleys and much low and swamp lands, capable of yielding good crops after thorough drainage. The first settlers were Messrs. Housey, of Housey's Rapids, Joshua Long, Robt. Benn, Brass (two families), Brooks (two families), Wyle. Mr. Wyle is father of the first white child born in the township. There are eight or nine German families in Ryde. Seven years ago (say 1872) there were no settlers. Five years ago Ryde came into market. There is a good winter road to Bracebridge, but Gravenhurst is the natural business centre. After the Rusks (two brothers), Daney and Matz (three families), had settled in Ryde they did not know each other's places of residence. Messrs. Downie and Long were settled five miles apart, and each unknown to the other. They came in by different routes about six years ago. Downie hearing some one chopping, met Long, and found that he had a near neighbor, and that there was a road to Bracebridge.

MACAULAY.

Macaulay (chiefly important as containing Bracebridge) contains 38,639 acres of land, and 1,341 of water. It is practically out of the market as a free grant township, but improved farms are to be occasionally had at reasonable rates. Several important roads (to Baysville, Huntsville, Gravenhurst, etc.) radiate through the village. A bridge is needed near the High Falls, as settlers at opposite sides of the north branch of the Muskoka River have to make a detour through Bracebridge to visit each other. The Muskoka Lake and River are also utilized as means of transit by the settlers, there being a large number of private boats of various kinds in use, besides Mr. Cockburn's daily steamers. Macaulay, agriculturally, is best suited for pasture, unless near Bracebridge where market gardening will increase with the growth of the village. The manufacturing facilities of the township are unrivalled, the number of water privileges has been computed at 200, but without claiming so high a number, it may safely be said that a number of most excellent water privileges exists in Ma-

caulay, Bracebridge Falls, Halstead's water privilege in the village (at present unutilized), Willson's Falls, the various branches of the High Falls, South Falls, Tretheway's Falls, etc., the water supply being almost always constant, and the supply practically unlimited.

Falkenburg, on the main road to Huntsville, at the junction of the Parry Sound Road, is a village in Macaulay, five miles from Bracebridge, and containing two hotels, an Anglican Church, saw mill and shingle mill (belonging to Mr. M. Moore), and blacksmith's shop.

BRACEBRIDGE.

The length of the following description of Bracebridge may provoke surprise, if not adverse comment from the English reader, to whom a population of ten thousand clustered together would seem insignificant, and who cannot conceive how a village of twelve hundred people could deserve anything more than a passing notice. Scores of such villages can be found in England, with an apothecary, a pettifogging attorney to set neighbors by the ears, a store with a few clay pipes, a little cheese, and a post office window, whence letters are slowly dispersed by some old woman to the public as they stand outside in the rain. Time seems to make little impression for better or for worse on such fossil English villages, no new enterprises start up, and the village is a stereotyped finality. But Bracebridge is a centre, the importance of which is not measurable by its present population, but rather by the rapidity with which it increases, and the nine solid pillars (hereafter described) on which the prosperity of the village is built.

1. Bracebridge, in the first place, has excellent water privileges at the falls, which at present support a grist mill and woolen mill, and might support six good-sized factories if fully utilized. In addition to this great fall there is a less one still within the village limits suitable for a small factory. The supply of water is practically unlimited and unfailing.

2. Bracebridge is the terminus of navigation on the Muskoka River. Note what this involves: arrest of transit, transhipment, teaming, and of the business created at a central distributing point. There are only two apparent dangers in the future to the traffic, one the possible erection of locks to evade the falls; the other, the building of a railway passing through Bracebridge, and piercing the heart of the back country without break or halting place.

The first danger to the trade of Bracebridge we may leave for the consideration of the men of the next century. The amount of rock to be blasted and the extent of lockage required to overcome the obstructions of the Bracebridge Falls, Halstead's Rapids, Willson's Falls, and the High Falls, would render the canalization of the north branch impracticable for many a long day, though not to be refused admission among the possibilities of a distant future.

The second danger—the fear of Bracebridge being "killed" by the passage of a railway near the village, and going north—is a vivid bugbear in the minds of a few timid speculators. The majority of our citizens, however, do not fear the snorting of the iron horse. Even as to the local traffic now carried by steamers to the port of Bracebridge, it would be in accordance with the analogies of the development of trade elsewhere if, eventually, a larger steamboat traffic than ever was the result. True it is that as Huntsville and other local centres to the north of Bracebridge enlarge and multiply, they will take a certain portion of the Bracebridge trade away. Even now some storekeepers who have business connections in Orillia or Toronto, team their goods directly from Gravenhurst station. On the other hand new settlers are pouring in every day, and on the whole the business of the village is steadily and rapidly increasing. The older established firms in Bracebridge do not seem to suffer from the competition of the newer ones, and often the difficulty, especially in hardware, is to keep stock enough to supply the demand, the telegraph being often called in to stimulate the speedy arrival of new goods. A railway would create a market which does not now exist, for hard wood, pressed hay, and other commodities. It would also immensely increase the value of real estate both in Bracebridge and the country through which it passed. On the whole the danger of Bracebridge being killed by a railway may be dismissed as a chimera.

3. Bracebridge has a central position with respect to the district of Muskoka. It is not the geometrical centre but it is the centre in a very practical sense of the population of the district of Muskoka, and of large portions of that of Parry Sound.

4. Hence its eminent suitability for a county town, taken in conjunction with the fact that it already possesses the registry office for the whole district of Muskoka, the division court and lock-up; the registry office and lock-up having been built well and substantially of brick, by the Ontario Government.

5. It is the point of confluence and divergence for the travel and business of the greater part of Muskoka, and a large portion of Parry Sound; the townships of Ryde, Oakley (greater portion), McLean, Macaulay, Monck, Draper (greater portion), Muskoka (a little), McMurrich, Ryerson, Perry, Franklin, Chaffey (a good deal, especially in good sleighing), Wood and Medora (in winter), Watt and Cardwell (a good deal). In the winter Parry Sound Harbor is closed by ice, and every one coming into either Muskoka or Parry Sound must pass

through Bracebridge (some small travel by Bala excepted). From Bracebridge radiate roads to Huntsville, Baysville, Gravenhurst, Parry Sound, etc. These great roads are fed by lesser tributaries, which form a complex and ever-extending net-work of travel.

6. Bracebridge is the religious, educational, literary, and journalistic centre of Muskoka, and, to a very measurable extent, of Parry Sound. It is the residence of the Roman Catholic Bishop, the headquarters of the Canada Methodist and Presbyterian Churches. In the last named system the Bracebridge pastor has jurisdiction over Parry Sound. In Bracebridge the examinations for Muskoka teachers and the semi-annual school conventions are held, while the largest newspapers in the two districts are published here.

7. Saw-mills excepted, Bracebridge is the only manufacturing centre in the two districts, having two tanneries, one of which is the most perfect on this continent, woolen mill, grist mill, planing mill, and a large sash and door factory is about to be erected in a few months. Events foreshadow a very large increase in the number of these and other industries.

8. Bracebridge has got the start so far as manufacture and trade are concerned. Every commercial man knows how hard it is to displace an old centre of business, which has already made its connections, and spread its mercantile roots far and wide, to bring nourishment to the parent tree. A stern chase is proverbially a long one, and were the quoting of authorities needed we might quote the great Charles Babbage, in the "Economy of Manufactures," who there shows that a manufacturing centre, from the mere fact of its being the first in the field, can hold its own against younger rivals, equally favored in other advantages.

9. The ruling men in Bracebridge are shrewd, go-ahead men, making mistakes of course sometimes, but on the whole keenly alive to the interests of the village, and not likely to throw chances away. This they proved by giving a two thousand dollar bonus to the Beardmore tannery.

The village also taxes itself heavily for the support of the Fire Department. Almost every Muskoka enterprise, whether it be a cheese factory or a provisional County scheme, originates in Bracebridge, where also is the centre of political caucuses of both political creeds. The Muskoka people look to Bracebridge to take the initiative in every great social, political, or religious movement, and they do not look in vain.

It is hard to lay one's finger on the exact moment of the birth of the village. We may first name James Cooper (father of Joseph Cooper, saw-mill owner and councillor, of Bracebridge), who squatted on land which is now included within the village limits. James Cooper's land included both sides of the Falls. Alexander Bailey bought out Cooper's claim in 1863. Messrs. Perry & Myers bought out from Bailey. John Beal and David Leith squatted about the same time, and, together with James Cooper, were the pioneers of Bracebridge. In 1861 Bracebridge consisted of the log huts and potato patches of Messrs. John Beal and David Leith, James Cooper's log house, and a small brick tavern and store, built on the south side of the river (there being no bridge save a large pine tree, which spanned the Falls) by Hiram Macdonald. James Cooper built a tavern in 1865, at which time there was only a weekly mail to what is now Bracebridge. In 1866 two or three little bush stores were carried on by Gilman Willson, William Holditch and Hiram Macdonald, also a frame store, built by A. H. Browning in the bush (as it then was), and Joseph Cooper's frame house on the main street. Then Mr. John Teviotdale's arrival gave the village an impetus, since he built the first large substantial store in the village. Mr. Teviotdale till his death continued to be a prominent citizen, and made large improvements of the village, where his widow now resides.

Mr. Teviotdale, the son of a farmer in Morayshire, Scotland, after a mercantile training in Glasgow, set sail for Canada at the age of 21 years. He remained four or five years in Cobourg, where he married; he spent some years in Hastings and Peterborough, and came to Muskoka in 1867, his health having broken down, and his desire being to retire to a small place, where he could find just enough business to keep his mind employed. In the words of his biographer, in the *Free Grant Gazette*, " his own energy created a business of such magnitude as to demand all his attention, and his time was soon fully monopolized, as it would have been in the hum of city life."

After about six years of Muskoka life, Mr. Teviotdale offered himself as an independent candidate at the general election for the Commons. He was also the nominee of the Conservative Convention before the last election for the local house. He died on September 16th, 1875, aged 42 years. About the time of Mr. Teviotdale's arrival in Bracebridge, Hiram James Macdonald built the store now occupied by Mr. Campbell on the hill overlooking the right bank of the river.

In 1870 Messrs. Perry & Myers came to the village from Whitby. Mr. R. E. Perry is a Canadian, and the son of the late Peter Perry, who represented the County of Ontario in the old Parliament, and his brother is the present registrar of Whitby. Mr. R. E. Perry has been subsequently Reeve of Bracebridge, and Warden of the County Victoria.

Mr. T. M. Myers is a native of England. Messrs. Perry & Myers, after their arrival in Bracebridge, bought out Bailey's property, consisting of saw mill and grist mill, with one hundred acres of land, part of which is now within the village limits, and largely built on. The price was six thousand dollars, and the purchase included the whole water power of the falls, which they now retain, with the exception of the portion sold by them to Mr. Bird, the owner of woolen mills. Subsequently, Mr. R. E. Perry bought the grist mill. At the time when Messrs. P. and M. arrived, there were about twelve houses in Bracebridge, and certainly not over one hundred people. Instead of over four large hotels, there was the old " Royal" and a log building, kept by G. F. Gow, where the "Dominion " now stands. People had to stage it to Orillia, about thirty-six miles, to make purchases. Messrs. P. and M. also bought out the stock, and rented the only store in the village from Mr. Teviotdale. Subsequently, Mr. Myers purchased the store itself and adjacent property. At that time, stages only travelled once a week to Parry Sound and Huntsville, the latter village then consisting of one or two houses. There were only the steamers *Wenonah* and *Waubamik* plying their trade on the lakes. There was no express office or telegraph. In the winter, goods were brought from Orillia in the summer, they had to be drawn up from the wharf in a one-horse sled, owned by Mr. Gow, there being no wheeled vehicle, and the sight was often witnessed of a merchant toiling through the slush up the hill from the wharf with a parcel of goods on his back. The Methodists worshipped then in the Orange Hall, while their minister, Rev. S. B. Phillips, lived in part of a small stable, with a quilt for a window. In the autumn they built a Methodist parsonage. Messrs. Clerihue (partner of Mr. Hunt) and Dill arrived not long after Mr. Myers, and do a large business now in the village.

To show the change wrought by improved means of communication, let it be mentioned that in these early days salt cost $4.00 per barrel instead of $1.35, its present price, and a keg of nails $7.00, but now $3.50. Our space will not allow the chronicling of various other arrivals in the village. Suffice it to say that the old mercantile settlers to a great extent remain and flourish. The solvency and credit of Bracebridge stands high in the commercial agencies, there having been very few failures of importance. In 1870 the first newspaper was established in the village, namely, the *Northern Advocate*, which the proprietor, Mr. McMurray, transferred from Parry Sound to Bracebridge.

In 1872 the population of Bracebridge was about 500, and on Oct. 6th of the same year St. Thomas's (Anglican) Church (24 x 48 feet, with 60 feet spire) was opened for service. Various interesting events, such as the visit of the Press Association, and of Lord Dufferin in 1874, occurred between our last epoch and 1875, the date of the incorporation of the village.

In 1876 the leading event was the unanimous voting of a bonus of two thousand dollars to Messrs. Beardmore Bros., of Toronto, on condition that they should build their new tannery in Bracebridge. The tannery was accordingly built in the following year, and is described as it now exists in another part of this article. Suffice it here to say that the Beardmore tannery is—if not the very largest—among the largest in Canada, and admittedly the most complete on this continent in its arrangements and machinery. Before building the tannery, Messrs. Beardmore got the plans of the tannery of Messrs. Jewett & Keating, in Port Alleghany, which was supposed to be the *ne plus ultra* in the United States. They also visited that tannery, and noted the comments of the proprietors as to certain minor defects which actual working showed to exist in it. Aided thus, and by their own experience, they have founded the model tannery of the continent.

At the beginning of 1877, a school census showed 269 scholars between the ages of five and twenty-one years, in the village school section, most of them under sixteen years.

The Beardmore tannery was exempted by the council from taxation for ten years.

The new Registry Office, a substantial brick building with fire-proof vault, was finished by the contractor, Mr. Neil Livingstone. The cost was borne by the Ontario Government.

The Mechanics' Institute gave a series of entertainments during the winter, including a most attractive lecture on combustion, by Mr. Bird, in which the lime light was shown by a new generator, invented and manufactured by Mr. Bird.

Violets were in full bloom in Mr. Myers' garden on February 22nd.

A sale of municipal and fire debentures took place in Toronto, the price realized being 92 cents on the dollar, cash.

The auditors reported $2,068 collected for the year 1876-7, of general taxes, and only $18 uncollected, a result which spoke well for the solvency of the village. The total receipts, including special rates and license fees, etc., was $2,291.25. The village assessment for 1877 was $118,605, being an increase of $25,535 over last year, and the amount of "non-resident" lands was reduced from $4,520 for 1876, to $2,600. On July 6th the Mayor and Corporation of the City of Toronto visited Bracebridge, and were presented with an address by the village council, to which a suitable reply was given by the Mayor.

Let us glance at the existing institutions and public societies of the village:

The Mechanics' Institute began existence in 1874, with a library of 225 volumes, and now, aided by a Government grant of $400, has secured a library of 700 volumes, including the American Cyclopedia, which cost nearly $100. Mr. Aubrey White has long and efficiently acted as honorary secretary, and Mr. Josiah Pratt is the painstaking and courteous librarian. Scientific and literary entertainments are given under the auspices of the Institute, and it is affiliated to a literary debating society.

The fire company (Rescue No. 1) comprises some fifty members, who wear a handsome uniform. There is a strongly built and powerful hand engine, together with 550 feet of hose, hose reel, &c., and a lofty bell tower, with large fire bell. The establishment of the company and the purchase of the engine was the result of considerable energy on the part of the people. In 1876 a baker's shop was burned down in the principal street of the village, and before the embers were cool a requisition was handed to the Reeve for the summoning of a public meeting to arrange for purchase of engine, &c. The Council, before submitting a by-law raising $1,500 for that purpose to the voters, summoned a public meeting to test the popular feeling, and finding themselves unanimously sustained, they framed a by-law to raise $1,500 for engine, &c., which became law, and large additional sums were subsequently spent on the fire department. Mr. James Boyer framed an excellent code of fire company by-laws, and was the first Secretary, being succeeded by Mr. W. E. Hamilton, and being now again the Secretary of the Company, of which Mr. John Adair is Chairman and Mr. John Haw, Captain.

The Winter Evening Amusement Association has been in existence more than four years, and under the able leadership of Mr. Burden (proprietor Queen's Hotel), has collected an excellent company of local amateurs, who give dramatic entertainments of a high order during the winter season, the Shakespearian drama having been represented to an appreciative audience in 1878.

The Masonic Lodge (Muskoka Lodge, No. 360) meets on the Tuesday on or before each full moon. The dispensation under which the Lodge works was received from the Grand Lodge of Canada in the spring of 1877, and the warrant granted in the fall of the same year, with W. R. Bro. Isaac Huber, as Master, a position still acceptably filled by him.

The Orange Lodge, L. O. L. No. 218 (W. Willis, Master; Richard Mills, Deputy Master; T. D. Speer, Chaplain; G. T. Graffe, Secretary; James Boyer, Financial Secretary; Joseph Cooper, Treasurer; James Clark, Director of Ceremonies; Hugh Stevenson, First Committeeman; John Glover, Treasurer), has been established about nine years, meets on the second Friday in each month, contains about 45 members, and is parent of three other bodies, which have branched off from it, namely, those of Stoneleigh, Monck, and the Junction.

A first-class cricket club is organized to play on the grounds of the Agricultural Society.

A base-ball club is also in existence, also a bowling alley, and two billiard tables, where champion matches are played with Gravenhurst.

The Agricultural Society of Muskoka and Parry Sound, though not exclusively a Bracebridge society, holds its annual meeting and supper in the village, and has its own fenced-in grounds and agricultural shed on the village outskirts. It is in a flourishing condition, having a good surplus on hand, after paying all expenses.

The Beaver Temple (I. O. G. T.) has a lodge in Bracebridge, and has been in existence for several years, but seems now to be torpid, if not defunct.

The remaining societies are the Bible Society, Temperance Association, Chess Club (games are played annually by telegraph with Huntsville, two of which have been published in the *Globe*), Cricket Club, and General Improvement Society. An Oddfellows' Lodge is in process of formation.

The following comprise the churches :—

The Anglican Church (St. Thomas')—Rev. J. S. Cole, incumbent (also in charge of out-lying stations at Falkenburg, Stoneleigh and Bardsville), stipend about $850; Churchwardens, Messrs. W. E. Foot and W. Kirk; Vestry Clerk, Mr. Hanks; Beadle, W. Gibbs. Services—Matins, 10.30 o'clock; Sunday School, 2.30 o'clock; Evensong, 7.00 o'clock. Buildings, etc.—Church, with spire and bell, Sunday School house (20x40), mortuary, chapel, and cemetery.

Canada Methodist Church—Rev. W. T. Hewitt, pastor; Recording Steward, E. F. Stephenson. Hours of service —Morning, 10.30 o'clock; Sunday School, 2.30 o'clock; evening, 6.30 o'clock; prayer meeting every Thursday evening; class meetings on Sundays and Tuesdays. Rev. Mr. Hewitt is Chairman of the Muskoka District.

Presbyterian Church—Rev. A. Findlay, pastor (salary, $700); has charge of thirty-three stations, which he inspects twice a year. The new church was formally opened Dec. 17, 1876, in presence of Hon. John McMurrich and other notables. It cost about $3,000. It measures 51x34 feet, with tower 79 feet high. Hours of service—Morning, 10.30 o'clock; evening, 6.30 o'clock; prayer meeting, 7.30 o'clock, Thursdays.

Primitive Methodist Church—Rev. G. F. Lee, pastor. Hours of service—Morning, 10.30 o'clock; Sunday School 2.30 p. m.; evening, 6.30 o'clock.

Roman Catholic Church (St. Joseph's)—Ecclesiastics, His Lordship Rt. Rev. Monseigneur Jamot, Bishop of Sarepta, and Rev. P. Cody, P. P. High Mass, 10.30 a. m.; Catechism for children at 3 p. m.; Vespers at 4 p. m. Bishop Jamot, who takes his title *in partibus infidelium*, has his headquarters in Bracebridge, whence he makes his missionary tour through Muskoka, and in the summer travels through Algoma. Value of church property in Bracebridge, $4,500.

There are in the village 2 hardware stores, 6 general stores, 7 groceries, 1 drug store, 1 photographer, 2 flour and feed stores, 3 bakers, 3 butchers, 3 tailors, 1 book and variety store, 2 milliners, 6 dressmakers, 1 watchmaker and jeweller, 1 cooper, 1 saw mill, 1 planing mill (a little outside the village), 5 tinsmiths, 7 painters, 26 carpenters, 4 wheelwrights, 3 blacksmith shops, 10 blacksmiths, 3 waggon shops, 2 tanneries, wharf, wharf house, and grain store, 2 newspaper and job offices, 6 printers, 3 editors, 3 conveyancers, 3 auctioneers, 5 solicitors.

The official directory of Dominion Government officials is as follows :—

Postmaster—R. E. Perry. (In winter, not only all the mail matter for the whole District of Muskoka and Parry Sound, but also for Algoma, comes to the Bracebridge office.)

Post Office Savings Bank—4 and 5 per cent. allowed on deposits, with Dominion Government security.

Money Order Office—At Post Office. Orders issued and cashed on or from offices in Dominion, U. S., Great Britain and Ireland.

Fishery Inspector—W. E. Foot. (Fishery licenses granted.)

Official Assignee—T. M. Bowerman.

The following is the directory of Ontario Government officials :—

First Division Court—Held six times a year. His Honor C. W. Lount is the Division Court Judge.

Clerk—Thomas M. Bowerman.

Bailiff—Robert H. White.

Stipendiary Magistrate—His Honor Judge Lount.

Gaoler—Robert H. White.

Justices of the Peace—The Reeve, *ex officio*, James Clerihue.

Constables—W. J. Hill, J. H. Tomlin.

Registry Office—(Brick building with fire-proof vault, built by Ontario Government.) Registrar, J. Ewart Lount. In this very important office, original conveyances, mortgages, etc., affecting property in the District of Muskoka proper, are preserved, searches made, etc.

Crown Lands Agent—Aubrey White (who succeeded Judge Lount.) At this office applications are received for locations, cancellation of transfers and patents, under the Free Grant Act.

Immigration Agency—The territory to which immigrants are forwarded from this Agency includes that of the Crown Lands Agency, together with a portion of Parry Sound. In the winter, immigrants going to any part of the two districts (Gravenhurst and the portion between Gravenhurst and Bracebridge excepted) pass through the Bracebridge Agency. In addition to his official duty of advising immigrants, the agent endeavors to obtain employment for them, and corresponds with intending settlers in various parts of Europe.

Immigration Agent—W. E. Hamilton, B. A. T. C. D.

Government Woodrangers—A. Judd, D. F. Macdonald, —. Shaw.

Tavern License Department — The Commissioners (Matthias Moore, Chairman, —. Beley, and J. P. Cockburn), are appointed by the Ontario Government, and grant all licenses in Muskoka and Parry Sound.

License Inspector—E. F. Stephenson.

Coroners—Samuel Bridgland, M. D.; W. Rear, M. D.

Issuers of Marriage Licenses—3.

Commissioners in B. R.—5.

Registrar of Vital Statistics—James Boyer.

Municipal Council—Reeve, John Smith; Councillors, E. F. Stephenson, T. M. Bowerman, Joseph Cooper, James Langdon; Clerk, James Boyer.

Caretaker of Fire Engine—John Adair.

Bellringer—W. Slater.

Fire Warden—John Adair.

Sanitary Inspector—James Boyer.

Assessor and Collector—Robert H. White.

Public School—Head Master, Seymour Eaton; Assistants, Miss Martin, Miss Adair, Miss Oaten; Caretakers, —. Glover, —. Phillips.

Montreal Telegraph Company—Agent, S. Bridgland, M. D.; Operator, Walter Foot; Wire Inspector, Robert H. White.

Vicker's Express Co.—Agent, F. W. Dill.

Muskoka Navigation Co.—Solicitor, J. B. Browning; Wharfinger, Robert Oaten; Deputy Wharfinger, Julian Oaten.

Manufactures—Saw mill, Joseph Cooper; grist mill, R. E. Perry; woolen mill, H. F. Bird; tannery (local hides) Jonas Bowman; tannery, Beardmore Bros., General Manager, —. Willson.

DRAPER.

There are here 41,758 acres of land and 927 of water. Reported as very well situated in regard to water and mill privileges, the Muskoka River flowing through the township, upon which there is abundance of power. It contains the village of Muskokaville or South Falls, which was originally surveyed by the government as a town plot, and contains post office, church, school-house, store, and several private houses. Bracebridge has, so to speak, killed the South Falls Village, where, however, there is a magnificent water power of a total descent of 130 feet in 1,000 feet of length.

Matthiasville is an excellent site for a village (see illustration), containing a church for all Protestant denominations (built at the sole expense of Mr. Matthias), shoemaker shop, blacksmith shop, saw and grist mills, and the residence of Mr. Matthias and his son. There is good trout fishing here in the season at the falls on the south branch of the Muskoka River.

The township is still joined to Oakley for municipal purposes, but separated from its former municipal companion "Ryde." The Council for Draper and Oakley for 1879 is as follows: Reeve, Rob. McMurray; Councillors, Wm. Bennett, Michael Cooke, Timothy Patterson, and James Smith.

Draper was organized in 1868, with Thomas McMurray as Reeve, the amount of assessment being $2,700; number of persons, 363; cattle, 170; sheep, 93; horses, 18. In 1869 the assessment was $19,520; cattle, 194; sheep, 88; horses, 16. In 1871 the assessment was $21,919, and in 1872 it had risen to $31,479. In 1873 it was $43,250; population, 488; cattle, 450; sheep 85; horses, 31. In 1876 the assessment was $55,910; population, 640; cattle, 542; horses, 67. In 1877 the assessment was $60,683; population, 675; cattle, 867; sheep, 292; horses, 80. In 1878 the assessment was $64,056; population, 750; horses, 168. It will be noted that the assessed value of property per head has increased eightfold in ten years, while the population itself has more than doubled.

OAKLEY

contains 43,884 acres of land, and 3,011 of water. Within the last eighteen months the immigrating public are beginning to appreciate this township, which would have been filled up years ago had it not been reserved under timber limits, which, however, did not bar the ingress of squatters. It is a good township for many reasons, and D. M. Card, Esq., the Inspector of Government Roads in Algoma and Muskoka, told the writer that he had hunted in conjunction with a party of friends over that part of the township which was condemned in the official survey, and that he found much excellent land there. There is good oak in the township. Besides the near markets of Bracebridge and Gravenhurst, the Toronto and Nipissing railway extension from Coboconk is surveyed to pass through Oakley, in which township, or in its immediate vicinity, a railway station is likely to be built.

M'LEAN

contains 37,544 acres of land and 4,600 of water. Mr. Burns, P. L. S., who surveyed in 1862, reports very favorably of the soil and the various water privileges which exist on the Muskoka River, which intersects it diagonally. A few free grant lots are still to be had. A steamer now runs during the season of navigation from Baysville to various points on Trading Lake and the Lake of Bays. Baysville seems destined to grow into a thriving village, being near the centre of McLean, and the point of confluence of three important roads. Lumbering operations also will extend annually further and further north, on streams of which the head waters lie near the Ottawa. Baysville is also a good centre for tourists, sportsmen and anglers, who like salmon trout, partridges, ducks and deer. Echo Lake, not far from Baysville, boasts seven places where seven first-class echoes are heard.

Baysville contains a grist mill, saw mill, shingle mill, wharf, three stores, school-house, where P. Methodists and Presbyterians worship, and, say, 25 inhabited houses.

The early settlers are Brown, Dickie, Bastedo, and the Langford's. The Indians used to do all their trading at Bigwin Island, with Bigwin, an Indian, who exchanged furs for provisions. An Indian chief's daughter and several other Indians are buried on the island. Cedar pickets whittled off with a jack-knife show the place of the graves, amid cedars and poplars. A window sash, whittled out with a jack-knife and regularly morticed, which was found amid the remains of an Indian house, prove their ingenuity.

RIDOUT

contains 33,785 acres of land and 3,779 of water. "The land is high and rolling; the whole township is covered with the finest description of timber; the western and north-western portions cannot be excelled for agricultural purposes." So says the Government surveyor, Mr. Rykert, who surveyed Ridout in 1862.

FRANKLIN

has 31,624 acres of land and 7,977 of water. It was placed in the market in 1877. It is well watered, contains a sufficient amount of pine, cedar, etc., for the wants of settlers, and water power to drive grist and saw mills. Mr. Marsh has a saw-mill in the Township. Franklin is rapidly settling up, and will probably be, in a few years, an important township.

MONCK.

Monck contains 27,835 acres of land, and 483 of water, is one of the oldest settled townships, and is practically out of the free grant market, but has some valuable farms for sale. It is an excellent agricultural township, and contains farms which would do credit to older settlements, some fine farms being in the immediate vicinity of Bracebridge. The township has the important advantage of frontage to Lake Muskoka and the Muskoka River. A steamer calls at Point Kaye on Muskoka Lake, twice weekly, and also at Tondern Island, the residence of Messrs. Prowse and Wilmot.

WATT

has 35,226 acres of land, and 12,057 of water. The Parry Sound Road passes through the township, which is considered one of the best for agricultural purposes in the Muskoka District. It has a frontage on Lake Rosseau, the steamer calling daily at Windermere Wharf.

Dee Bank Village in this township contains store, hotel, saw and grist mill (the latter one of the largest in the district), school, and other buildings.

The building now occupied as a Post Office at Ufford was, if not the very first school-house in the Muskoka District, at least the first north of Bracebridge. Mr. H. W. Gill, the present postmaster at Ufford, was the first teacher. The school building was commenced in 1866 and finished in 1867. Mr. Gill drew the first Government grant for school purposes north of Bracebridge.

There is good sporting in Watt, e. g., Mr. John L. Shea killed eight deer last season in this township.

STEPHENSON.

contains 42,973 acres of land and 3,262 acres of water, the land being "generally of a good quality south of the Seventh Concession," according to the surveyor's report, which also alludes to indications of the occasional presence of iron in the soil. Almost all the lots are taken up. The village of Utterson has a store, blacksmith shop, a large hotel, well conducted by Mr. Collins, and a well-built C. M. Church, with stained glass windows, also a town hall. There is a daily mail to Bracebridge, with daily stages.

Port Sydney, on Mary's Lake, is a most charmingly situated village. Here tourists can find a comfortable and well-kept hotel, whence they may make most enjoyable boating excursions along the picturesque shores of Mary's Lake. The Anglican Church, in the village, a large gothic edifice, furnished with stained glass windows, is a lasting monument to Rev. Mr. Cooper, through whose exertions mainly the church was built. Port Sydney has also a public school, several good private residences, a large public hall, in which amateur dramatic performances are given with great effect, and got up regardless of expense; also a grist mill, oat meal mill, saw mill, and some good stores. It is reached from Huntsville in the summer by the "Northern" steamboat, and enjoys a tri-weekly mail from Bracebridge, with a daily stage in the summer.

S. Anson. Del.

AMONG THE ISLANDS ON LAKE JOSEPH.

BRUNEL.

There are here 41,206 acres of land, and 3,437 of water. The rocky land is set down as about one-seventh of the whole. All the available land in the township appears to be located.

CHAFFEY.

Chaffey contains 46,236 acres of land, and 4,039 of water. It is a well watered township, with good mill sites on the East River, and abundance of excellent land.

The important village of Huntsville, in this township, is situated on the stream connecting Fairy and Vernon Lakes. It is about 25 miles from Bracebridge, by daily stage in the winter, and in the summer the journey is made via steamboat to Port Sydney, and thence per stage to Bracebridge. There is also a tri-weekly stage to Katrine and Ernsdale. In Huntsville there are three churches (Presbyterian, Anglican and Canada Methodist), public school, Orange Hall, temperance lodge, doctor, printing and job office, weekly newspaper (*The Forester*), telegraph office, freight office, two hotels, five general stores, hardware store, butcher, shoemaker, tailor, milliner and dressmaker, harness shop, two blacksmiths, seven carpenters, a pump and wagon shop, and two saw mills. Mr. Hunt erected a bark-roofed shanty in the then unbroken forest nine years ago, where Huntsville now stands, and this shanty was the gathering place "of the clans" for all secular or religious meetings.

STISTED.

We find 43,014 acres of land, and 3,168 of water in this township. There are no large pine tracts, but a good deal of "scattering pine" through the hardwood, which is, as generally happens in such cases, of good quality. Aspdin Village has two stores, two churches (one being Anglican), post office, and school-house, with accommodation for travellers at one of the stores. At the old site of Stanleydale there are an Orange Hall, and four houses. Ilfracombe is a new settlement which has progressed with amazing rapidity since the first commencement of farming work in the spring of 1877. It is composed of gentlemen of good position and means from England. They have made large clearings, and expect to have an Anglican Church built and endowed soon with funds procured from England.

MEDORA.

There are 41,619 acres of land, and 21,911 of water in this township. It has a large water frontage on the three principal lakes of the district, Muskoka, Rosseau, and Joseph, and is the favorite resort of tourists. The

scenery and fishing in this township are unsurpassed elsewhere in the district. It is bounded on the south by the Muskoka River, the outlet of Muskoka Lake, celebrated for its bass and maskinonge fishing, and the romantic scenery between Muskoka Lake and the Georgian Bay. For agricultural purposes it is not so good as many other townships, being so much cut up by the lakes, the shores of which are generally rocky. There are, however, some good farms in the township.

At Port Sandfield is a canal between Lakes Rosseau and Joseph, to allow the steamer access to the latter lake. Here is a bridge built by the Ontario Government at great expense. It is about 60 feet above the water level. The numerous beautiful islands on Lakes Rosseau and Joseph have been bought by wealthy residents of Toronto, and other towns in the Front, who, in many cases, have erected summer residences thereon, in which they and their families can spend their summer holidays in boating, fishing, and other amusements, in perfect independence and retirement not to be had at the hotels.

The township contains the village of Port Carling, where there are Anglican, Canada Methodist, and Presbyterian Churches, two stores, two saw mills, school-house, post office, and a good hotel. It is one of the daily ports of call for Mr. Cockburn's steamers, and is a very convenient spot for tourists, being centrally situated with respect to the Muskoka, Rosseau, and Joseph Lakes. Boats and guides to the splendid fishing grounds in the vicinity can be had on application to Mr. Thomas, proprietor of the North Star Hotel. A steam yacht of light draught, suitable for tourists and anglers, can be hired on reasonable terms on application to John Rogers, Port Carling. The locks here were built at great expense by the Ontario Government to allow steamers to get up to Lake Rosseau. The township was incorporated in 1871 (including the Township of Wood). J. D. Cockburn was the first reeve. Mr. Burgess, of Bala, is now and has been for some years reeve of the municipality.

WOOD.

Wood embraces 62,776 acres of land and 5,491 of water. Mr. Scott, who surveyed it (in part) in 1870, says: "There are two excellent tracts of land, . . . The balance of the township is much broken and very rocky, and almost totally unfit for agricultural purposes. There is good water power at each of the three chutes of the Muskoka River." It is one of the largest townships in the district, and has an extensive water frontage, being bounded on the north-east by Muskoka Lake, on the south by the Severn River, and on the north by the Muskoka River. The township is incorporated with Medora for municipal purposes.

EAST PARRY SOUND AGENCY.

The Agency contains three townships, viz.: McMurrich, Armour, and Perry. The agent is Edward Handy, Esq., Elmsdale, Township of Perry, eighteen miles from Huntsville. (See map.)

M'MURRICH.

McMurrich contains 38,787 acres of land (of which about 13,000 were reported as still open for location in 1877), 3,324 acres of water and 838 of roads. Now, however, nearly every lot suitable for settlement has been taken up. According to the report of Mr. C. F. Miles, P. L. S., the greater portion of the township is composed of open, rolling hardwood land, with a certain portion of tamarack, spruce and cedar swamps, very wet in some places. The soil is also reported by the same authority to be a good sandy loam in the uplands, and a rich black loam in the lowlands. "The timber is distributed in the following order and quantity, viz.: black birch, which grows to a large size, maple, hemlock, balsam, pine, spruce, tamarack, cedar, ironwood, basswood, elm, and oak." "The township is watered by numerous small streams, running into Axe Lake, Round Lake, and Buck Lake, the former two emptying into the latter, and ultimately into the Muskoka River." "While the lakes are open, access can be had from the south by way of the Stephenson (Muskoka) Road, Vernon, Fox, and Buck Lakes, with two short portages; from the north by way of the River Maganetawan and Doe Lake, into the north-east corner of the township."

So much for the official reports, but to wind up the description of McMurrich, while ignoring Mr. A. Begg, the founder of the settlement, would be to give Hamlet with Hamlet's part left out.

This energetic son of an energetic race, small in stature, but of a large brain and tireless limbs, is one of those restless beings to whom a residence for a year in the same place would be agony. On some hot summer's day he may be encountered, perched upon the stage wagon between Bracebridge and Port Sydney, gracefully festooned, like a Grecian deity, with fern leaves, which hide every feature except the genial and humorous eye peeking through the cool canopy of verdure. In a few days he dates from Orillia. A few weeks pass, and he is in London, England. He next turns up in Bracebridge, collects specimens of beasts, birds and minerals; advocates the cause of Muskoka at the Paris Exhibition, comes back to Canada with salmon ova, tramps many a weary mile through Northern Muskoka, and is again seen among the list of Canadian arrivals in London.

Such a wanderer, keenly enjoying a joke, full of energy, pluck and new ideas, is Mr. A. Begg, the pioneer of

McMurrich, native of the north of Scotland, near John o'Groats' House. He has been settled in Canada since 1846. From 1871 to 1875 he was engaged in promoting emigration from Scotland to Canada. He was applied to by temperance men to select a suitable tract for them on which to settle. In 1874 he selected McMurrich, which was then entirely unoccupied. In the fall of 1874 and spring of 1875 he cut roads, built a saw mill and a shingle mill, adding a grist mill, and establishing a post office at Beggsboro' in 1876. The original programme of reserving the township for temperance people was not carried out, and the Ontario Government threw open the township to all comers, though at first the arrivals included a large number of business men. Mr. Begg expended much time and money in getting the township opened up. He brought out at his own expense a civil engineer from Toronto to report on the soil and capabilities of the district, which report appeared in the Toronto papers. He has now lived to see the partial fruition of his labors,—roads, large clearances, good crops, and three post offices in what was in 1875 a waste howling wilderness. Such is the transformation effected by the pluck, energy and endurance of a man working at an age when most of us court repose.

PERRY.

Perry contains 46,334 acres of land (of which two-thirds are officially reported as being fit for settlement), and 1,610 of water. Mr. Chapman, P. L. S., reports good water privileges on the Maganetawan, and as to agriculture, he considers that while hay, turnips, oats, and the coarser cereals thrive well, stock raising would be the most profitable.

ARMOUR.

Armour contains 40,655 acres of land, and 3,350 of water. The soil on the high lands is officially reported as sandy loam, while the soil of the valley of the Maganetawan is a rich clay loam. Below the forks of the Maganetawan is Burke's Falls, possessing a good mill site, and seems destined to develop into a thriving village.

RYERSON

contains 45,908 acres of land and 2,812 of water. Mr. Clementi, who surveyed it in 1870, designates the soil as "generally of a sandy loam, light on the immediate surface, but becoming more rich as you dig deeper, with a fine subsoil of clay. . . . I consider there is seventy per cent. of arable land in the township." The rocky aspect of the lake shores, so forbidding to an explorer, gives place to smoother land as he recedes from the water.

This township has gained a wide notoriety in connection with what might be called the "Donaldson Colonization Scheme." Mr. Donaldson's plan was that the Ontario Government should clear five acres on certain suitable lots in a selected township, and erect a house thereon ; that they should sell this partially improved lot to the small capitalist for $200, and that he should still be liable to perfect the balance of his settlement conditions by the clearing of ten additional acres, and by residence for the otherwise prescribed period of five years. This admirable plan had for one essential feature that this payment of $200 should be *in cash* before the settler got possession. Thus the cash received from the sale would be put into circulation again immediately for the clearance of another similar lot. This essential *cash* element was ignored in the clearing and locating of the lots in Ryerson, and hence, the original scheme having been mutilated, and the Government thrown into the false position of a small creditor (with the usual result of not getting paid its claim), no unfavorable inference can be logically drawn from the comparative failure of the actual experiment, as against the original and complete "Donaldson Colonization Scheme." Fifty-eight families, however, have been located upon improved lots in the township, and one hundred families on unimproved lots.

PARRY SOUND AGENCY.

This agency contains ten townships, viz.: Cardwell (in Muskoka District), Carling, Christie, Ferguson, Foley, Hagerman, Humphrey, Monteith, McDougall, and McKellar. The agent is Mr. Thomas McMurray, Parry Sound Village, in the Township of McDougall.

CARDWELL.

Cardwell is within the limits of the Muskoka District, though included in the Parry Sound Agency. It contains 46,275 acres of land, of which but a small part is located. There is a good stream in the township called the Rosseau River, having several good mill sites, and a saw mill at the outlet on Rosseau Lake.

HUMPHREY.

Humphrey contains 35,654 acres of land, and 12,496 acres of water (Lakes Joseph, Rosseau, etc.), has a good water privilege at White Oak Creek, and has a great variety of timber, some of very large size. All the usual crops of the district have been cultivated with success, and although a considerable portion of the township is unfit for settlement, yet there is excellent land to be found on the higher levels for agriculture, and on the lower flats for pasture, which includes the natural and nutritious blue joint of the beaver meadows.

The early settlers were Mr. Sirett and his family, Geo. Milne, Mr. Williams, Edward Clifford, John Lorimer, Richard Irwin, and James Ashdown.

In the township of Humphrey are the villages of Rosseau (Helmsley), Ashdown, and Port Cockburn.

The village of Rosseau comprises three stores, two hotels, saw mill, boot and shoe maker, telegraph office (at Pratt's Hotel), post office, express office, and schoolhouse, besides Anglican and Presbyterian Churches.

The Rosseau House, better known perhaps as Pratt's Hotel, deserves special mention, being the largest in the district and widely known to tourists. The enterprising proprietor (who is an American) has constructed a steamboat landing for the use of his guests, and makes annual enlargements and improvements of his premises, so as to make the hotel finally, if it is not at present, the largest and best hotel north of Toronto in this province. Visitors will find here the comforts of a first-class city hotel, combined with the bracing atmosphere and beautiful scenery of the Muskoka lakes, and will not generally be satisfied with a single visit.

Mr. Clifford squatted on the lots by the site of the present village of Rosseau in 1864. He sold his right and title to about four acres to Mr. Pratt, the proprietor of the Rosseau House. The village was surveyed in 1866, and Mr. Clifford left and took up another lot. Mr. C. was the first settler in the township, and the first settler between Skeleton River and Parry Sound. He now lives on the next lot to the village plot. Mr. Sirett was one of the first settlers in Humphrey, having arrived in 1864. He is Immigration Agent at Rosseau.

Ashdown contains a Canada Methodist Church, Orange Hall, store, blacksmith shop, carriage and wagon shop, and post office. It is situated at the junction of the Parry Sound and Nipissing Roads.

Port Cockburn has a large hotel called the Summit House, aptly so named, and is a popular resting place for the wearied tourist, whence very picturesque lake vistas through the trees, and refreshing breezes, are enjoyed by the visitor, whose creature comforts are earnestly catered for by the obliging host, Mr. Fraser.

Lake Joseph is generally considered by visitors to be the superior of the three lakes for fishing and scenery. It certainly has the advantage of having perfectly clear water, the waters of the other lakes being generally of a dark color, Muskoka Lake water especially being very dark.

Equity Crest, a bold headland (marked on map) on the west shore of Lake Joseph, in this township, was named by some gentlemen of the long robe in honor of Chancellor Spragge, on the occasion of his visit.

MONTEITH.

Monteith may be divided into 46,373 acres of land and 2,169 of water. Considerable settlement has progressed along the Rosseau and Nipissing Road. The south-eastern and north-western portions of Monteith, comprising about half the township, are reported as of rich sandy loam with clay subsoil, and good farming lands. The traveller will find an excellent temperance hotel at Seguin Falls, the proprietor of which, Mr. D. F. Burk, is a most genial and hospitable host, nor should we forget to praise the excellent *cuisine* of his good lady.

CHRISTIE.

Christie contains 43,954 acres of land, the greater portion of which is of good quality.

FOLEY.

Foley was surveyed in 1866 by Mr. Stewart, P. L. S., contains 36,043 acres of land, with 5,554 of water, and 910 acres of roads in 1877. "A large proportion," says the surveyor, " of this township is occupied by water, a characteristic common to this portion of the Province. The lakes throughout the township are generally very irregular in outline, presenting bold, rocky shores, and great depth of water. An examination of the map will show their position and extent. It will be observed that, towards the western portion of the township, they become more numerous and irregular, as we approach the Georgian Bay. These lakes present scenery of singular beauty and variety, and possess many attractions to the sportsman and tourist. The hills throughout the township are generally rugged and rocky, presenting in some cases impassable barriers. There are no large tracts of good pine found in the township, though occasional groups of very excellent red pine may be found throughout the hardwood tracts, worthy of the attention of the lumberman. Oak of good quality may be seen in various parts of the township, and birch is very abundant generally. . . . There were strong indications, however, in many places, of iron ore, and the effect on the magnetic needle was very troublesome, at times causing a variation of as much as fifteen or twenty degrees. I was not able to discover anything resembling ore on the surface, or samples would have been forwarded." Since the date of this report, a large vein of iron ore has been found in the vicinity of Otter Lake, which may at no distant date develop a valuable industry and source of profit to some enterprising capitalist.

Among the pioneer settlers may be named Mr. William Wilcox, Thomas McGown, William McPhillmay and William Scott, who have been successful in establishing comfortable homes for themselves out of the former wilderness.

Parry Harbor (formerly "Carrington") is the capital, so to speak, of Foley. It contains a saw mill, planing mill, shingle mill, two hotels, a store, school house, a Roman Catholic Church, two blacksmiths' shops, a wagon and carriage shop, post office, and telegraph office.

A very important institution in Parry Harbor is the Guelph Lumber Company, which commenced operations in 1873. They cut annually eleven million feet of saw logs, and employ seventy men around the mill. The logs come down to the mill on the Seguin River from its head waters and tributaries. They have a store, blacksmith's shop, shingle factory, telegraph office, and boarding house in connection with their mill. This extensive lumbering industry is under the management of George McLean. They have a steam barge of their own, *The Vanderbilt*, which makes regular trips from the mill yard to Sarnia and Duluth. In the winter they employ 160 men, exclusive of local jobbers. The Company own 250 square miles of timber limits, comprising the townships of Spence and Monteith, together with parts of Hagerman, McKellar, Ferguson, Christie, Shawanaga, Humphrey, and Foley. They have an extensive lumber yard in Sarnia, supplying the western peninsula of Ontario with lumber. Ever awake to the extension of their business connections, they have opened another lumber yard at Emerson, Manitoba. For this trade they have an extensive planing and dressing mill at Parry Harbor, and the dressed lumber is shipped via Duluth.

McDOUGALL.

McDougall contains 35,521 acres of land, and 4,420 of water, is situated on the Georgian Bay, and was surveyed in 1866. Certain agricultural drawbacks are compensated in a great measure by its facilities for the water transit of saw logs, and by its unrivalled possession of the port of Parry Sound, around the shores of which the village of the same name is built, which at no distant date will be developed into a town of no small importance. The village will be described separately, but as to the lumbering facilities, it may be added that the Seguin River is a very important artery of saw log driving, fed immediately by Mill Lake, at the foot of which the Messrs. Beatty have erected a dam, the chute being ten feet high.

The early settlers of Parry Sound and McDougall are Messrs. Wm. Beatty, Alfred Burritt, William Bowers, Thos. R. Caton, Frank Strain, and D. F. Macdonald. Mr. D. F. Macdonald, to whom the writer was indebted for valuable data in his former publication, and who has also most cordially furnished information for the Parry

Sound portion of this atlas, is a thorough explorer, and probably knows the whole Parry Sound district, from actual inspection, better than any other denizen of its confines.

PARRY SOUND VILLAGE.

The village and surrounding settlement are of very recent origin, although the harbor and locality were known to the early Jesuit missionaries who visited the Georgian Bay in the seventeenth century. An interesting relic was lately found within a few miles of this place, having cast in the metal the date 1636. The harbor and coast were surveyed nearly 50 years ago by Capt. Bayfield, at the same time that he surveyed the rest of the Georgian Bay and Lake Huron. He probably gave the name of Parry Sound to the beautiful body of water in the locality, and from which the village derived its name.

The first enterprise established here was that of Messrs. J. & W. Gibson & Co., of Willowdale, who erected a saw mill and commenced the manufacture of lumber in 1857. In 1863 they sold their mill and timber limits to Messrs. J. & W. Beatty & Co., of Thorold, who immediately commenced active operations.

In 1865 the Township of McDougall was surveyed, and the Parry Sound Road commenced. The steamer *Waubuno* was built in this year and opened steam communication between Parry Sound and Collingwood. The village of Parry Sound was soon after surveyed in town lots, and building operations have gone on actively since that time.

In 1872, J. & W. Beatty & Co. sold their timber limits and saw mill to Messrs. H. B. Rathburn & Son, who immediately sold it again to Messrs. A. G. P. Dodge & Co., who organized the Parry Sound Lumber Co. (Limited). In 1877, J. C. Miller, Esq., purchased the interest of the Messrs. Dodge in the Company, and is now the chief proprietor and active manager of that Company.

The population of the village is about 800. The trade, especially in summer time, is very active. About twenty-five million feet of lumber are annually shipped from this port. There are now about twelve stores of all kinds, some of which are doing a very large trade. The grist mill owned by Mr. Beatty is in active operation. There are three churches and three resident ministers. There are among the societies of the place a Masonic Lodge, Odd Fellows' Lodge, Orange Lodge, Orange Young Briton's Society, and a Good Templar's Lodge. There is a weekly newspaper (*North Star*) published by Thos. McMurray, Esq. There are also two public halls, a court house, jail and registry office, and public reading room.

The large saw mills are among the chief attractions of the place, as well as the chief means of its support. The large mill of the Parry Sound Lumber Co. has a capacity of over twelve millions annually, the Seguin Mills (owned by Mr. Wm. Beatty) a capacity of over five millions, and that of the Guelph Lumber Co. of about eleven millions. Parry Sound has unusual facilities for trade and commerce. The harbor is among the finest in the Dominion. There is ample water power to drive all sorts of machinery. A tannery, foundry, and a woolen factory would find a good opening here.

The annual camp-meeting which is held here brings together hundreds of both whites and Indians for worship. Parry Sound is rapidly becoming a favorite resort for summer tourists, as the scenery is unusually attractive and the climate salubrious.

The government have made free grants of lands in the surrounding country, and have an agent at Parry Sound. There are also a customs officer, immigration agent, Indian agent, registrar, and stipendiary magistrate located here.

FERGUSSON.

According to Mr. Fitzgerald's survey in 1869, it contains 31,837 acres of land, and 3,110 of water. The lakes are of clear good water, well stocked with the fish usually found in the Georgian Bay or Lake Huron.

The early settlers were Samuel Botteral, John Lamb, Geo. Van Camp, Louis Stiller, Hugh Shields, Richard Harrison, and Mr. Teneycke.

The village of Waubamik is situated in this township, and comprises post office, carpenter's shop, and store.

McKELLAR VILLAGE.

McKellar Village is the second halting place, about sixteen miles on the great highway of travel to the Northern Townships from Parry Sound. Here the traveller gladly stretches his wearied limbs at the McKellar House, and after all his carnal wants have been fully supplied by the genial host, Mr. William Thompson, he takes a bird's-eye view of the charmingly located village, between Owl and Minerva Lakes. The goddess of wisdom and her symbolic bird must surely have assisted the founders of the village in the selection of its site, so as to combine the elements of commercial convenience and beauty of landscape. From the north and south portions of the great north road, streams of travel converge on the village, while yet another feeder is afforded by the east road, which leads to Spence. The two latter, which surround the village, united by a short stream now affording water power for a grist mill and saw mill, and which can be utilized in the future for other industries, give another outlet for the transit of settlers and their merchandize. On the lower lake sail boats, canoes, and scows are in full operation, and the trade of McKellar is swelled by the settlers so arriving.

The tourist will find the McKellar House a home in every sense of the word. The host, without fussy obsequiousness or fidgety and obtrusive worrying, contrives to make the guest feel perfectly at ease before he has been many hours housed in the hotel, and boats are at his command for fishing or general idling on the lakes. The business traveller finds quiet and prompt attention, and reluctantly leaves this cosy hostelry for the unknown regions of the north.

The writer, who lived in McKellar in 1874, on seeing a drawing of the village, from which that embodied in the present atlas is reproduced, felt perplexed which to admire most, the fidelity of the artist, or the gourd-like growth of the village during the last four years. It was like seeing the photograph of a full-grown youth after years of separation, and recognizing the old expression of features while viewing, for the first time, the stalwart limbs and expanded muscles which marred the recognition of identity.

The writer spent a very enjoyable time in McKellar (the frame only of the above-mentioned hotel was then in process of erection) in the autumn of '74. Grotesque incidents cropped up thickly during his stay. To try to reproduce some of them seems almost like offering his readers uncorked champagne after the sparkling aroma has fled. Let me begin by warning them against inferring anything discouraging against the fishing prospects of McKellar from what follows. Ill luck as an angler seems to be my destiny from the cradle to the grave. If there be truth in astrology, I was never born under the constellation *Pisces;* fish may play about my hook, and even commit petty larceny on the bait, they will do everything but get hooked, and even then the line snaps as a rule, so that I write "without prejudice," as the lawyers say, to the trout and pickerel fishing, which is excellent. To resume. I fished, as in duty bound, with my usual tantalizing result of catching nothing, with a costly fishing rod (lancewood end joint, patent reel, &c.), while adjacent urchins were hauling out their scaly victims hand over hand. As a last forlorn hope I tried Armstrong's scow, which was moored alongside the bank of the lower lake, as a fishing platform. An eight-year old McKellarite initiated me into the secret of getting irresistible bait—the silver minnow, which appeared in shoals near the waste water of the mill. The *modus operandi* is to get a square shallow basswood sieve, and hold it quietly and steadily in the bottom of the water, while your confederate stealthily drops bread crumbs over it, whereupon the minnows, timidly at first, but afterwards in shoals, attack the bait. At this stage, a quick upward jerk of the sieve, and lo! a sieve-full of struggling minnows, enough for a couple of hours' fishing. Armed with this bait, I fished for two hours from the scow. No sooner

was the hook dropped than a fish was seen darting at the minnow, which sparkled like molten silver through the water. In two hours I caught enough fish, when strung through the gills, to cover an eight-foot pole completely. I marched to the hotel in triumph. It is true that some of the fish were very small, but still the solitary exception to a life of angling ill-luck marked that day as a red letter day for all time. Its glory was somewhat dimmed by the looks of mild contempt cast by casual villagers, as they brushed against my up-lifted trophy. Entering the hotel, and expecting an ovation, I saw the McKellarites looking disdainfully at my spoils, and heard the words whispered, "only perch," in various tones of pity. In that region pickerel is only thought worthy of a true angler's aims. One critic went so far as to tell me that perch were full of worms in the fall of the year, though, worms or no worms, they are toothsome additions to the table. Taking this culinary view of the result, feeling that I had lost caste among the male part of the angling tribe, I retreated with my fish to the kitchen, seeking sympathy from the softer inmates of the tavern. Little did I know then that woman, culinary woman, dreads above all things the eviscerating of small fish. But here I was subject to fresh censure. Sun-fish were found in my collection, and though the catching of perch in a pickerel region may be winked at, the man who descends to catch sun-fish is beyond redemption. That evening eight feet long of perch might have been seen floating down by the mill, while the writer made a solemn vow never to fish for perch again.

One angling duty remained unperformed—to fish for pickerel. I visited a renowned pickerel *habitat* on the upper lake, below "Falls," which at that time resolved themselves into a very insignificant water-spout, and as usual caught nothing. The soft and solemn scenery of the lake, its pine-clad shores, deeply scalloped by bays of every fantastic shape, gave no small solace to the repining angler.

Reader, did you ever see a catfish? If not, bear with me for a few short sentences devoted to that monstrosity. I forgot to tell you that, while fishing from the scow, I saw something wriggling, grovelling, and stirring up the mud at the bottom of the water, presumably a fish, but possibly a musk-rat or an otter, for all I could tell. It snapped my bait off twice, with contemptuous jerks. At last I landed it safely and found that it was a catfish. I spared its life, and kept it in a bottomless barrel sunk in shallow water at the back of the hotel. One night a jovial gathering rejoiced "mine host," and lasted till the small hours of morning, when, about 2 P. M., somebody suggested supper. A foraging party assailed the larder. Tea and pork were unearthed, but no butter. I volunteered, then and there, to catch a fish, in the dark, as my contribution. They all stared, and jeered, after which I baited my rod and sallied forth alone, went to the barrel, and returned with a living and writhing catfish on the hook. Petrified by my swift nocturnal catch, and voting me a wizard of the first order, one of the party—on whom Bacchus had poured out his spirit abundantly, and on whom the lot had fallen to skin the catfish—set to work, knife in hand, to make the first incision. While so doing, it seemed to the excited toper as if the hideous scowl of this most repulsive fish followed him with such unwavering and magnetic sorcery that he feared to make the gash, dashing it down in terror, and leaving the task of dissection for another comrade. The cooked catfish had a delicious "meaty" flavor, which condoned its forbidding aspect. The Indian mode of cooking it is to leave the skinned fish previously for some hours in a swiftly running stream.

Deer-hunting along the lake shores was another pastime. Two hunters one day, with loud and ostentatious preface, recounting the boastful record of their past conquests in the chase, after the manner of the Homeric warriors, sallied forth. For brevity let us christen them (fictitiously of course) Jack and Mac. Mac was to row along the shore, while Jack and the dog were to start the deer towards the water. Soon we heard the loud shouting and the deep baying of the hound, that joyful utterance when he has struck the scent of the antlered monarch. The clear, frosty air sent each sound of the chase with almost painful distinctness through the interlacing foliage of the trees. Nearer and nearer bayed the hound, and then seemed to retrace its steps, as if the stag had doubled back to the forest. Meanwhile, a swift dappled vision appeared, some graceful animal in mortal terror, a ring of crimson gore circling its arched neck, and bounding with such fleetness over the cleared bottom land that the eye could just but identify it as a deer. Shades of Abbotsford, what a theme for your immortal owner! But, alas, something always spoils romance in America. The deer was Mrs. Samuel Armstrong's pet deer, and the ring of crimson gore round its neck was an identifying strip of red flannel, placed there by the fair owner.

Now for some dry statistics. The township of McKellar, surveyed into farm lots in 1869 by J. W. Fitzgerald, P. L. S., contains 44,755 acres. The surveyor's report describes the easterly half of the township as "considerably broken" (by which euphemism we suppose he means "very rocky"), with the exception of a good tract near Oliver Lake, and occasional oases along Manitowabin River. Pine is inferior in this easterly half, but enormous cedars, together with good-sized spruce and tamarack, are enumerated, while white oak is abundant. The last-named timber points to McKellar as a waggon building centre for the wide circle of country, to supply which waggon-makers in the front would be heavily weighted in the competition from the high freights to Parry Sound, and the comparative scarcity of good white oak in the older districts of Western Ontario. Of the easterly half of McKellar, 40 per cent., or say 8,500 acres, are reported by the surveyor as good land; the south portion of the westerly half contains "perhaps larger and thicker" oak than elsewhere, with good mill sites and 80 per cent. of land fit for cultivation. As to the easterly half, it is noted that the soil (generally clay) is more gravelly and stony on side hills, but deep and heavy in the valleys.

The first white settler in McKellar Township was Peter Leach, a trapper, who made this region his home in the summer of 1868, and still resides in the Township. David Patterson, who now occupies the very important position of Registrar of Births, Marriages, and Deaths, for unorganized townships, was the second bona fide settler, and the first in or near McKellar Village, and built the first shanty in the fall of 1868. Samuel and John Armstrong are the pioneers of this and the surrounding townships, started the first store, post office, saw mill, grist mill, shingle mill, lath mill, blacksmith shop, and were leaders generally in the development of the settlement, as they still continue to be. McKellar Township was incorporated in the spring of 1873, under a special Act of the Ontario Legislature, granting municipal institutions in unorganized districts without connection with any County Council. The first election for Reeve and Councillors was held in the Orange Hall, McKellar Village, on Thursday, the 1st day of May, 1873. Samuel Armstrong, Jr., was elected Reeve, and Wm. A. Hurd, James McKeown, George B. Lee and Samuel E. Oldfield, Councillors, holding office to the end of 1874. Mr. S. Armstrong has held the office of Reeve continuously up to the present time, and Mr. D. Patterson has worthily filled the office of Clerk for the same period. The first sitting of the Division Court for the District of Parry Sound was held in the store of S. & J. Armstrong, McKellar Village, on the 4th April, 1872, His Honor Judge McCurry presiding, with Henry Armstrong as Clerk, and but one case on the docket. Mr. Henry Armstrong is still Clerk, and Wm. J. Moffatt is the present bailiff. At the sitting of the Court in March, 1878, the docket showed a clean sheet, and His Honor earned the customary white gloves.

There are (for 1878) 160 ratepayers. McKellar Village consists of two stores, one hotel, one waggon shop, one grist mill, one saw mill, one blacksmith shop, two boot and shoe makers, one C. M. church, an Orange hall, school house and post office.

As history seldom does full justice to the early

pioneers of a new settlement, who are often subsequently bought out by wealthier successors, so that their very names fade away from public record, let us say that the McKellar pioneers included Mr. John Henley (who unfortunately lost his life in Manitowabin Lake by the capsizing of a canoe), Peter Leach, James Brownlee, James Buchner, Samuel Armstrong, Henry Moffatt, and Alex. Hardy.

HAGERMAN.

Hagerman contains 45,389 acres of land, and 3,577 of water. It is noted as containing excellent land and a peculiar limestone, the lime obtained from which will bear an addition of five or six parts of sand in mortar.

Mr. Geo. Kelcey, an English settler, who was a master painter and contractor in Rugby, England, settled here some years ago, and has now some seven hundred acres, and one hundred acres cleared. He may be called the founder of the village of Dunchurch.

Mr. Byrne's official report of Hagerman is said by some not to have done it justice; parts of it which he gave as containing 50 per cent. of good land having proved to be from 70 to 80 per cent. of excellent land when cleared up. For the first two years after it was thrown into the market, the land was taken up rapidly; after that time not so fast, as the land hunters as fast as they came into the district were advised by parties, from interested motives, to settle anywhere except up the north road, and hence few lots were taken up for the next three years.

The settlers who took up land when it first came into market have, without exception, done well. There are very few of them who have not from 30 to 40 acres cleared, Mr. George Kelcey (above referred to) having about 100 acres cleared. As a rule the settlers, owing to the excellence of the land, get their living from it, instead of at least partially depending on lumbering and other work for a livelihood. Being thus able to give their undivided attention and work to their farms, they are progressing rapidly. Though the townships south of Hagerman were longer settled, yet Hagerman was the first township north of Parry Sound to send grain to that market. The farmers have good buildings, stock, etc., and raise their own wheat and pork. The crops have never failed, excepting when the grasshoppers eat up everything except the beaver-meadow grass in 1872. The finest potatoes which the writer ever saw, either in America or Europe, were raised in Hagerman. Some of Mr. Kelcey's potatoes (early rose) were sent by the government agent to the Paris Exhibition.

The principal village in the township is Dunchurch, on the Northern Road, about 28 miles from Parry Sound. It contains (Dec., 1878) a store, post office, steam saw mill, blacksmith shop, and wagon-maker's shop, Union meeting house, Methodist Church, school house, &c.

A more beautiful site for a village than Dunchurch it would be difficult to conceive. Whitestone Lake consists of two parts, connected by a very narrow channel, over which the North Road, that great artery of travel from Parry Sound, crosses by the village bridge.

CARLING.

Carling is situate on Georgian Bay. Mr. Jas. Bolger, P. L. S., who surveyed it in 1873, reports 52,926 acres of land and 2,223 of water. "A little over a third part fit for settlement." The names of the early settlers are: Messrs. Robert Blair, John McNair, Finlaysons, Arthur Starkey, Joseph Cole, James Aloes, and ——. Morrison. Messrs. Moore & Atkins own a saw and shingle mill on "Syme's Creek," near the Georgian Bay, and have shipped lumber to ports along the Welland Canal.

MAGANETAWAN AGENCY.

This agency contains three townships:—Chapman, Croft, and Spence. Mr. S. G. Best, of Maganetawan Village, in the Township of Chapman, is Crown Land Agent.

CHAPMAN.

Chapman contains 45,486 acres of land and 3,120 of water, and is generally broken and hilly. Excellent crops of hay, oats, and cereals are raised, and command high figures from the lumbermen. At the foot of Se Sebe Lake are Miller's Falls, offering abundant and constant water power for manufacturing needs.

The progress of Maganetawan Village (see illustration) has been simply marvellous. The first necessity was some mode of crossing the river, and the first bridge across the Maganetawan was built on floating logs. A team crossing would sink the logs during the progress of transit, and the bridge recovered its level after the load had passed. This free and easy style of bridge has been replaced now by a permanent structure. To give some idea of the rapid progress of the settlement we may mention that a gentleman who visited Maganetawan Village in September, 1876, reported the existence at that time of one store and no hotels, in fact no stopping place except a sort of uncomfortable shanty, which gave free ingress to the winds of heaven. He also noticed Mr. Best's Crown Land Office, and Mr. Irwin's house. It had no appearance of a village. Now, there are two licensed hotels, four general stores, tin shop, baker's shop, watchmaker's, flour and feed store, school-house, and three churches, either built or in process of construction, whereof one (the Presbyterian) is to cost

LOWER CHUTE OF THE SOUTH FALLS.

$1,500. There are also private residences and a grist and saw mill, Crown Lands office, post office, and a temperance hotel. A steamboat (Messrs. Best & Walton, proprietors) runs daily during the season between Maganetawan and Burke's Falls, a distance of 23 miles, travelling through a well-settled country, on both sides of the river, including the best part of Ryerson, and some beautiful scenery near Se Sebe Lake. A second steamboat from the foot of Ah-Mic Lake to the Maganetawan is almost certain to be in operation in time for the opening of navigation in 1879.

CROFT.

Croft contains 44,866 acres of land, and 4,942 of water, has generally a soil of sandy loam interspersed with rocky ridges. There are several good mill privileges on the Maganetawan River, and on the north side of Ah-Mic Lake a splendid mill site with fall of 18 feet.

SPENCE.

There are here 48,358 acres of land, and 1,206 (an unusually small proportion) of water. There are several most excellent tracts of hard-wood land in this township, but the best lots, so far as accessibility is concerned, have been taken up. Farmers get very high prices from lumbermen for their produce. There are not any very good mill sites.

The embryo village of Dufferin has a saw mill, store, and hotel, and at the junction of the Ryerson and Nipissing Roads is Spence Post Office, good store, boarding house, and public school.

TOWNSHIPS IN PARRY SOUND DISTRICT NOT YET OPEN FOR LOCATION.

STRONG.

Strong contains 38,893 acres of land, and 5,530 of water. It will be noticed, on reference to the map, that nearly the whole of water area is comprised in one lake, a feature somewhat different from most other townships in the free grant district. Although not yet open for location it is fully settled, and has a good saw mill belonging to Mr. Nicholls. We are given to understand that the land generally is of good quality.

BETHUNE.

Bethune embraces 45,238 acres of land and 2,232 of water. The official report does not claim over from 30 to 60 per cent. of good land—a good quality of sandy loam.

McKENZIE.

McKenzie is north of Hagerman, surveyed in 1872-3 by A. B. Scott, P. L. S. It contains 43,844 acres of land and 4,991 of water. About 60 per cent. of the land south of the Maganetawan is reported as very fair agricultural land. The early settlers are Messrs. Connell, Mortimer, Wilkins, and Stringer.

GURD.

Gurd is situated north of the township of Machar. It contains 36,716 acres of land and 249 acres of water only. The village of Commanda, in this township, bids fair to become an important point. The Commanda District, embracing area of (say) sixty square miles, did not contain a dozen inhabitants in the summer of 1875, nor a dozen acres chopped. By the close of 1877 there was a population of 150, with about 200 acres chopped and cleared in the township of Gurd alone.

In 1878, village lots were selling in Commanda at from $20 to $75 for half-acre lots, and $500 was refused for a log house and half-acre lot. We understand that a good hotel is now in operation, as well as a store kept by Mr. Fryer.

NIPISSING.

Mr. Beatty's farm, near Lake Nipissing, can find few rivals in any part of Canada. It is composed of excellent land with good clay bottom. Mr. Beatty originally came in by the Ottawa and tributaries, having to portage his goods over the breaks in the "magnificent water stretches." He then utilized the French River and Georgian Bay route for getting in supplies, and now travels and teams *via* Bracebridge. He has undergone great privations, and deserves credit for venturing on what he entered it was a "howling" wilderness in the most literal and wolfish sense. He has partially received his reward, having sold hay to the lumbermen at from $35 to $50 per ton, and 80 cents to $1.00 per bushel for oats.

APPENDIXES.

No person shall be located for any land under this Act or said regulations, unless such person is of the age of eighteen years and upwards, nor shall any person be so located for any greater quantity than 200 acres.

Before any person is located for any land as aforesaid, such person shall make an affidavit, to be deposited with the agent authorized to make such location, stating that he has not been located for any land under this Act or under said regulations, and that he is of the age of eighteen years or upwards, and believes the land for which he applies or desires to be located is suited for settlement and cultivation, and is not valuable chiefly for its mines, minerals, or pure timber, and that such location is desired for his benefit, and for the purpose of actual settlement and cultivation of such land, and not either directly or indirectly for the use or benefit of any other person or persons whomsoever, nor for the purpose of obtaining, possessing, or disposing of any of the pine trees growing or being on the said land, or any benefit or advantage therefrom, or any gold, silver, copper, lead, iron, or other mine or minerals, or any quarry or bed of stone, marble or gypsum thereon.

No patent shall issue for any land located under this Act or under said regulations, until the expiration of five years from the date of such location, nor until locatee or those claiming under him or some of them, have performed the following settlement duties, that is to say : have cleared and have under cultivation at least fifteen acres of the said land (whereof at least two acres shall be cleared and cultivated annually during the five years next after the date of the location, to be computed from such date), and have built a house thereon fit for habitation at least sixteen feet by twenty feet, and have actually and continuously resided upon and cultivated the said land for the term of five years next succeeding the date of such location, and from thence up to the issue of the patent, except that the locatee shall be allowed one month from the date of the location to enter upon and occupy the land, and that absence from the said land for

in all not more than six months during any one year (to be computed from the date of the location) shall not be held to be a cessation of such residence, provided such land be cultivated as aforesaid. On failure in performance of the settlement duties aforesaid, the location shall be forfeited, and all rights of the locatee or of any one claiming under him in the land shall cease.

All pine trees growing or being upon any land so located, and all gold, silver, lead, iron, or other mines or minerals, shall be considered as reserved from said location, and shall be the property of Her Majesty, except that the locatee or those claiming under him, may cut and use such trees as may be necessary for the purpose of building, fencing and fuel, on the land so located, and may also cut and dispose of all trees required to be removed, in actually clearing said land for cultivation, but no pine trees (except for the necessary building, fencing and fuel, as aforesaid) shall be cut beyond the limit of such actual clearing before the issuing of the patent ; and all pine trees so cut and disposed of (except for the necessary building, fencing and fuel, as aforesaid) shall be subject to the payment of the same dues as are at the time payable by the holders of licenses to cut timber or saw-logs.

All trees remaining on the land at the time the said patent issues, shall pass to the patentee.

Neither the locatee nor any one claiming under him, shall have power to alienate (otherwise than by desire) or to mortgage or pledge any land located as aforesaid, or any right or interest therein before the issue of the patent.

No alienation (otherwise than by desire), and no mortgage or pledge of such land, or of any right or interest therein by the locatee after the issue of the patent and within twenty years from the date of such location, and during the life-time of the wife of the locatee, shall be valid or of any effect, unless the same be by deed in which the wife of the locatee is one of the grantors with the husband, nor unless such deed is duly executed by her.

Every patent to be issued for any land located as aforesaid shall state in the body thereof the name of the original locatee of the land, and the date of the said location, and that the said patent is desired under the authority of this Act.

On the death of the locatee, whether before or after the issue of the patent for any land so located, all his then right and interest in and to such land shall descend to and become vested in his widow during her widowhood in lieu of dower, in case there be such widow surviving such locatee, but such widow may elect to have her dower in such land in lieu of the provision aforesaid.

No land located as aforesaid, nor any interest therein, shall in any event be or become liable to the satisfaction of any debt or liability contracted or incurred by the locatee, his widow, heirs, or devisees, before the issuing of the patent for such land.

After the issuing of the patent for any such land, and while such land, or any part thereof, or any interest therein, is owned by the locatee or his widow, heirs or devisees, such land, part, or interest, shall during twenty years next after the date of such location be exempt from attachment, levy under execution, or sale for payment of debts, and shall not be or become liable to the satisfaction of any debt or liability contracted or incurred before or during that period, save and except any debt secured by a valid mortgage or pledge of such land, made subsequently to the issuing of the patent.

Nothing in this act shall be construed to exempt any land from levy or sale for rates or taxes heretofore or hereafter legally imposed.

ORDERS AND REGULATIONS

Made under "The Free Grants and Homestead Act of 1868," and "The Public Lands Act of 1860," by order of His Excellency the Lieutenant-Governor in Council, dated 27th May, 1869.

1. The quantity of land to be located to any person as a Free Grant, under "The Free Grants and Homestead Act of 1868," subsequently to the 23rd of January, 1869, shall be one hundred acres, but in case it shall be made to appear to the satisfaction of the Commissioners of Crown Lands that any person located or to be located as aforesaid, has not by reason of rock, lakes or swamp, one hundred acres that can be made available for farming purposes, the quantity located to such person may be increased in the discretion of the Commissioner of Crown Lands to any number of acres not exceeding in the whole two hundred acres, so as to make one hundred acres of such farming land ; and the male head of a family located, or to be located, under the said Act, since the said 23rd day of January, 1869, having children under eighteen years of age residing with him, may be located for in all two hundred acres.

2. Any locatee under said last mentioned Act, being the male head of a family as aforesaid, shall be allowed to purchase an additional 100 acres at 50 cents per acre cash at the time of such location, subject to the same reservations and conditions and the performance of the same settlement duties as are provided in respect of free grant locations by the 9th and 10th sections of the said Act, except that actual residence and building on the land purchased will not be required.

3. The right is reserved to the Crown to construct on any land located under the said Act, or sold as hereinbefore provided, any colonization road or any road in lieu thereof, or partly deviating from any government allowance for road ; also the right to take from any such land any wood, gravel, or other materials required for the construction or improvement of any such road without making any compensation for the land or materials so taken, or for any injury occasioned by the construction of such road, and such rights may be exercised by the Commissioner of Crown Lands, or any one authorized by him for that purpose.

4. Holders of timber licenses, their servants and agents, are to have the right to haul their timber or logs over the uncleared portion of any land located as a free grant, or purchased as before provided, and to make such roads thereon as may be necessary for that purpose, doing no unnecessary damage, and to use all slides, portages, roads, or other works previously constructed or existing on any land so located or sold, and the right of access to and the free use of all streams and lakes theretofore used, or that may be necessary for the passage of timber or logs, and all land necessary for such works is reserved.

5. All pine trees growing upon any land hereafter located as a free grant under the said Act, or sold under the preceding regulations, shall be subject to any timber license in force at the time of such location or sale, or granted within five years subsequently thereto, and may, at any time before the issue of the patent for such land, be cut and removed under the authority of any such timber license while lawfully in force.

S. RICHARDS,
Commissioner of Crown Lands.

APPENDIX B.

CLOSE SEASONS FOR GAME AND FUR-BEARING ANIMALS IN ONTARIO.

Deer, elk, moose, reindeer, or cariboo, cannot be hunted, taken or killed from 15th December to 15th September in following year.

Wild turkeys, grouse, pheasants, prairie fowl, or partridge, from 1st February to 1st October.

Quail, from 1st January to 1st October.

Woodcock, from 1st January to 1st August.

Plover, from 1st May to 1st November.

Snipe, from 1st May to 15th August.

Water fowl, which are known as mallard, grey duck, black duck, wood or summer duck, and all kinds of duck known as teal, from 1st January to 1st September.

Other duck, wild swan or geese, from 1st May to 1st September.

Hares or rabbits, from 1st March to 1st September.

Beaver, muskrat, mink, sable, martin, racoon, otter or fisher, from 1st May to 1st November.

No eggs of any of the birds above mentioned shall be taken, destroyed or had in possession at any time.

It is also forbidden to hunt or kill deer at any time for the purpose of exportation out of Ontario.

By Revised Statutes of Ontario, cap. 201, it is not lawful to shoot, destroy, wound or injure any bird whatsoever, save and except eagles, falcons, hawks, owls, wild pigeons, king fishers, jays, crows, ravens, and black birds, and the birds mentioned in the game list.

APPENDIX C.

CLOSE SEASONS FOR FISH.

White fish, salmon trout, lake trout, from 1st November to 16th November.

Speckled trout, brook or river trout, from 15th September to 1st May.

Bass, from 15th May to 15th June.

Pickerel and maskinonge, from 15th April to 15th May.

The above-named fish must not be fished for, caught, bought, sold, or had in possession during the close season.

With the view of affording better protection to fish in Trading Lake, and streams flowing into it, the south branch of Muskoka River, Black River, Seguin River, Maganetawan River, and their tributaries, parties angling for pleasure in such waters will be required to do so under Special Permits, in accordance with the Fisheries Act. These Permits may be had on application to W. E. Foot, Esq., Fishery Overseer, Bracebridge, to British subjects free, to other persons on payment of a small fee.

MAP OF MORRISON TOWNSHIP.
MUSKOKA

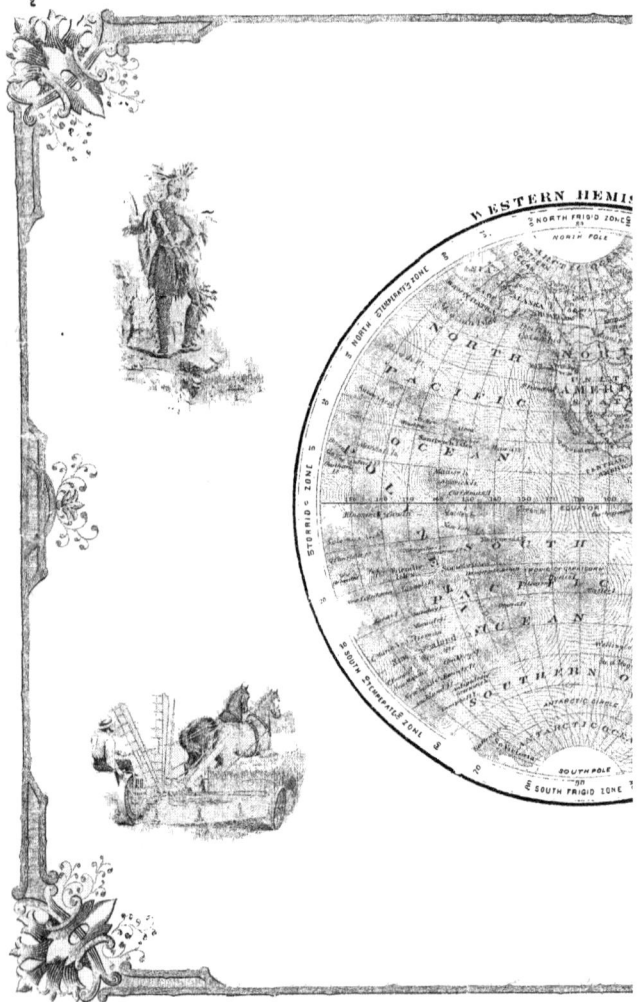

WESTERN HEMIS

NORTH FRIG'D ZONE

NORTH POLE

NORTH PACIFIC OCEAN

NORTH AMERIC

EQUATOR

STORRID ZONE

SOUTH PACIFIC OCEAN

SOUTHERN O

ANTARCTIC CIRCLE

ANTARCTIC OCE

SOUTH POLE

SOUTH FRIGID ZONE

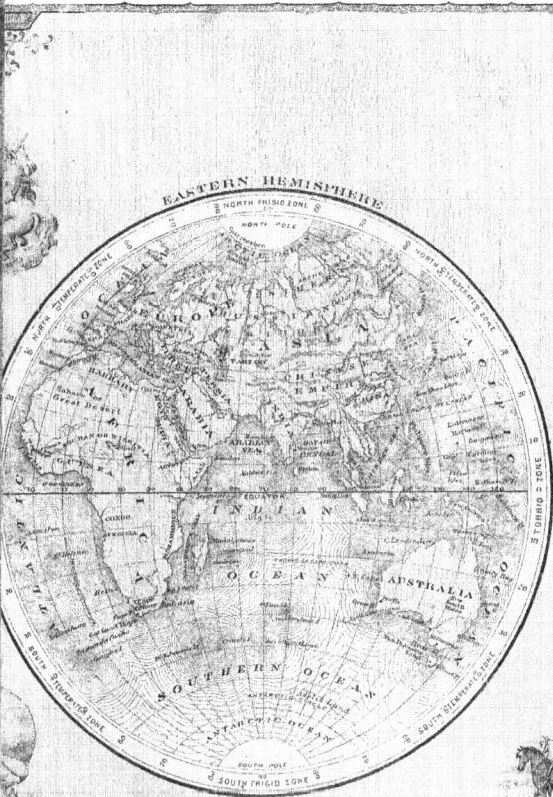

EASTERN HEMISPHERE

CANADA

MAP OF **RYDE** TOWNSHIP

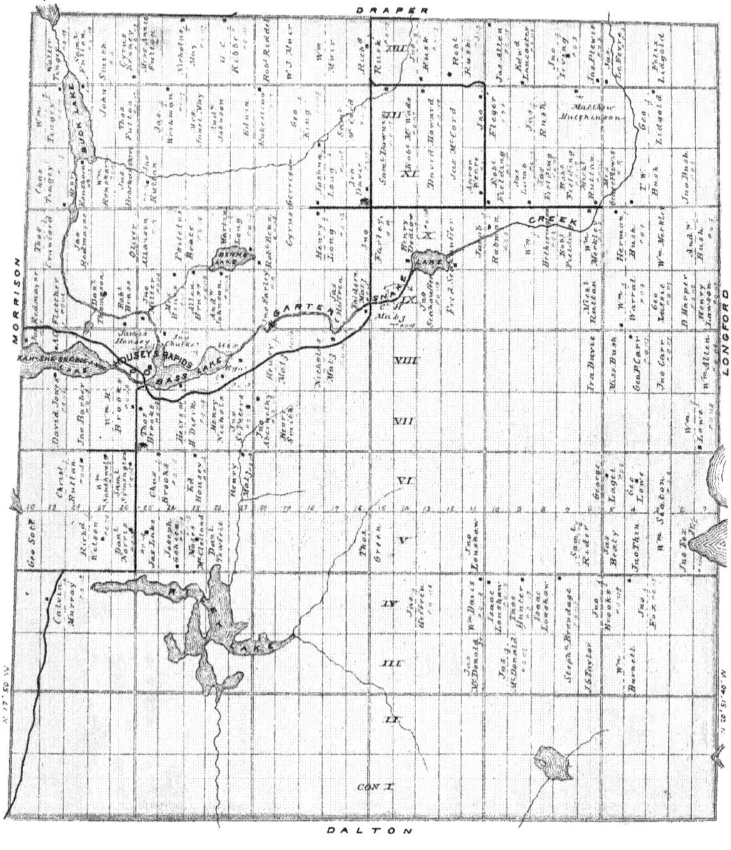

DRAPER
DALTON
MORRISON
LONGFORD
BUCK LAKE
KAH-SHE-SHEBOGAMOG LAKE
HOUSEY'S RAPIDS
BASS LAKE
GARTER
SNAKE
CREEK
CON. I
II
III
IV
V
VI
VII
VIII
IX
X
XI
XII
XIII

MATTHIASVILLE.

RES OF L.C.ROPER,ESQ, MARY LAKE.

RIVER STREET POULTRY YARD . W.W.GROOM,ESQ. PROP'R.

MAP OF DRAPER TOWNSHIP

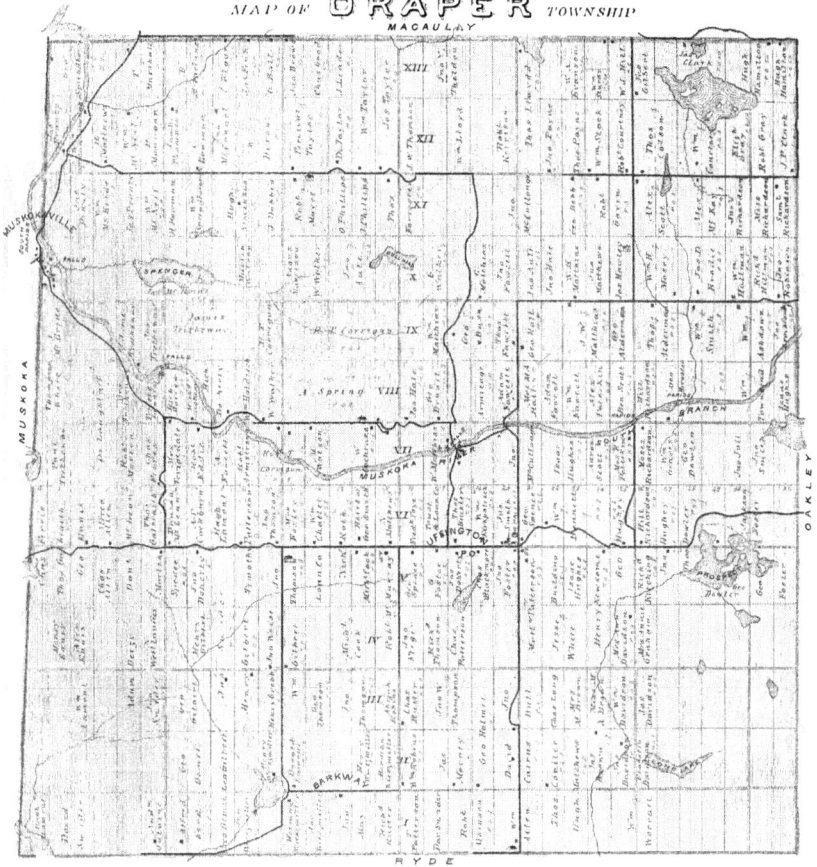

RIVER SEVERN
MORRISON LAKE
MORRISON

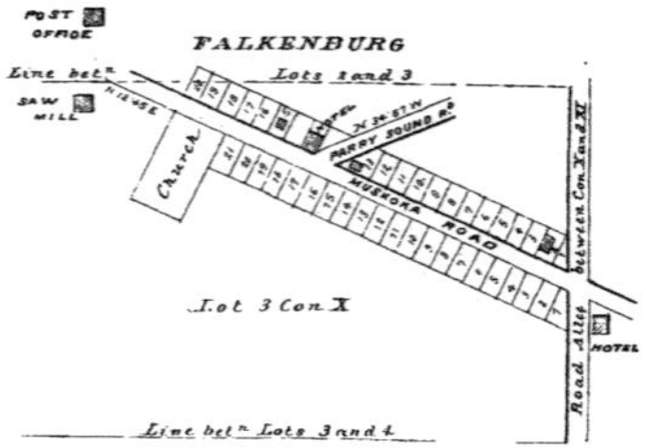
FALKENBURG
POST OFFICE
SAW MILL
Line betn Lots 2 and 3
Church
PARRY SOUND RD
MUSKOKA ROAD
Lot 3 Con X
Road Allow between Con X and XI
HOTEL
Line betn Lots 3 and 4

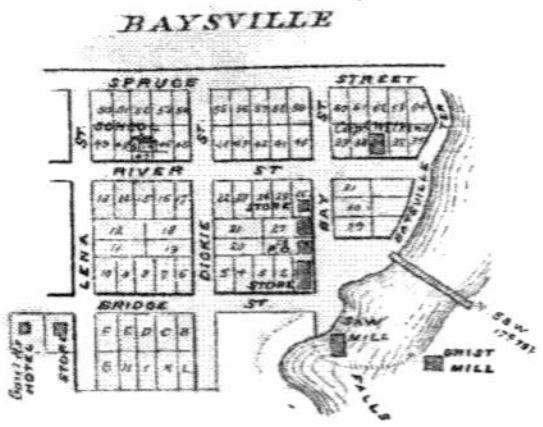
BAYSVILLE
SPRUCE
STREET
RIVER
ST
LENA
DICKIE
BAY
BRIDGE
STORE
SAW MILL
GRIST MILL
FALLS
HOTEL

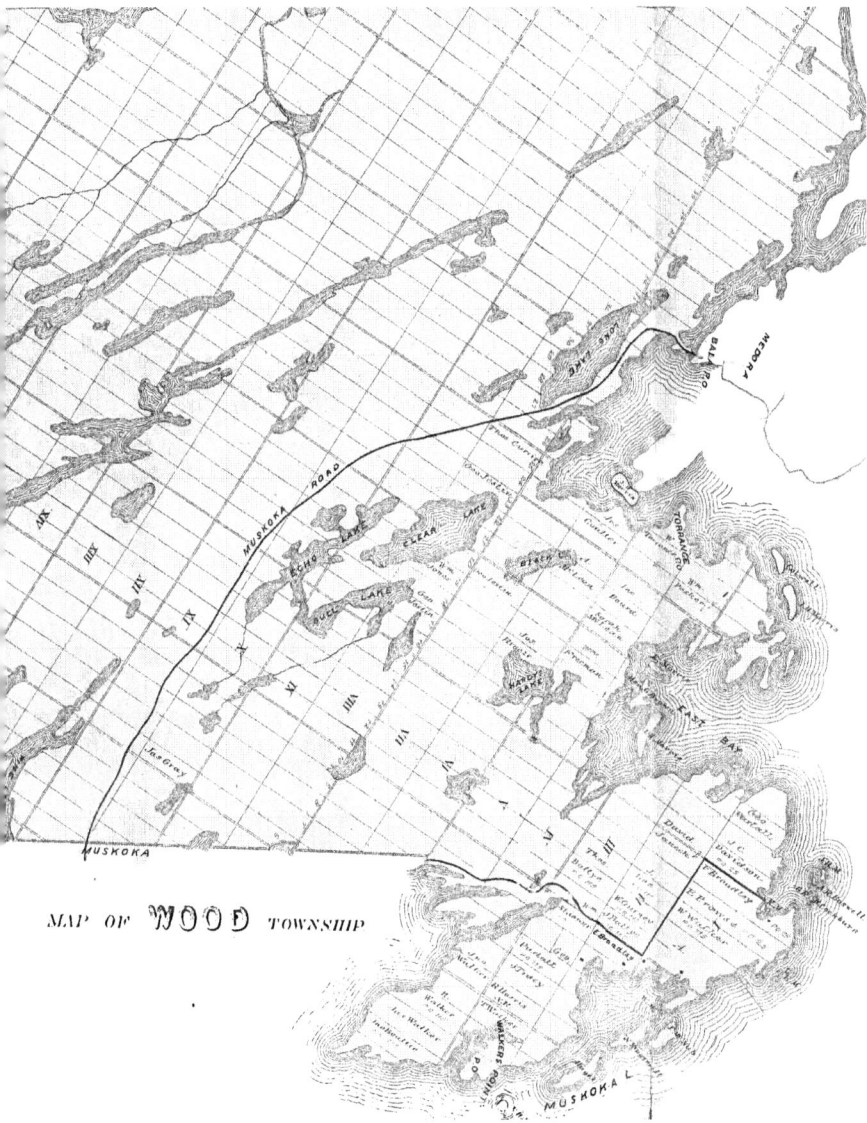

MAP OF WOOD TOWNSHIP

MAP OF OAKLEY TOWNSHIP

ON MUSKOKA LAKE

PORT CARLING.

MAP OF **MUSKOKA** TOWNSHIP

WOOD
MUSKOSH
RIVER
LAKE MUSKOKA
Glengarry Id
Camp Comfort Club
GLEN ORCHARD
BUTTERFLY LAKE
INDIAN RIVER
Renshaw
Dempster
Murphy
Michael Mooney
G. J. Mason
Jos Dempster
Chas Gaunt
Margaret Dempster
Arthur Gunne
Jno Ray
Jno May
Chas Gaunt
Selina Pegg
Alex Sutherland
Jno Graham
W. Hall
Edward Gostick
R. Burrall
Jas. A. Harsant
Angus McKay
Elizabeth McKay
Jno Owens
Alex Sutherland
Isaac White
Thos Hurrant
Andrew Anderson
Jno Nixon
Archibald McCollum
Jno Kelley
Henry Guy
West
Thos West
Fenn
J White
R Gilbert
Thompson
E.D.Stubbs
Albert May
Wm Lorway
Harry Waters
Thos Henshaw
Thos May
Anderson
D Dockstader
Samuel Brothers
R F Baker
Francis
Edward Cooper
W.H. Foreman
Geo Shouldice
W Foreman
Geo Carr
H James

DORA TOWNSHIP.

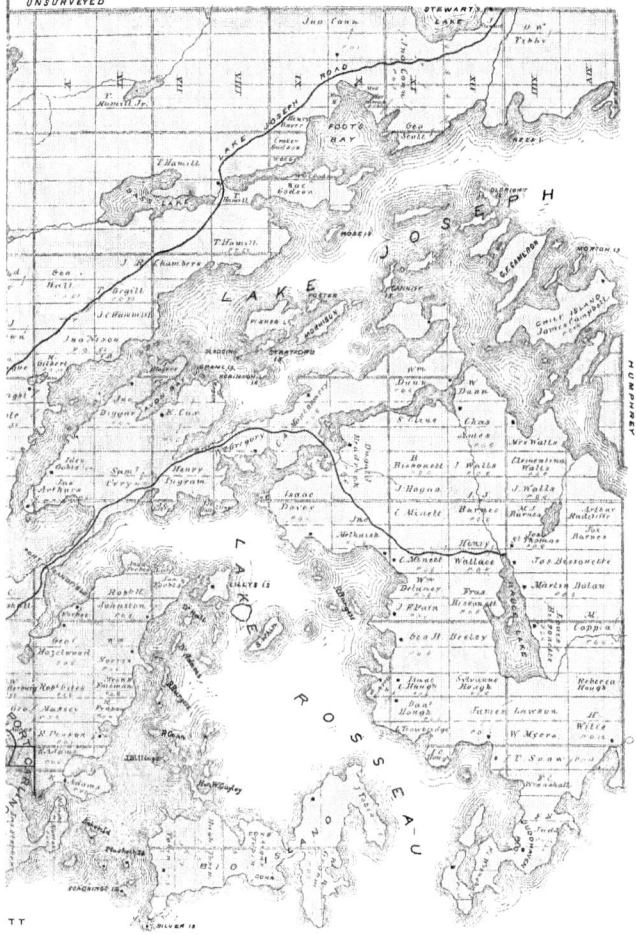

WATT

LAKE MUSKOKA

LEONARD LAKE

MEDORA

MACAULAY

CARDWELL

BARDSVILLE P.O.

XIII

XII

X

IX

VIII

VII

VI

V

IV

III

Wm Jack

Wm Bromley

Robt Howard

Ann Hamilton

Matthias Moore

Geo Moore

Fras Moore

Matthias Moore

Mary Hay

Edwd Hay

N. Kerby

N. Brown Jr

W Brown

Jos Lowe

Wm Burton

R. Whipp

T. H. Pope

Jno Coulson

Wm Tait

Jno McKay

Geo Coulson

Jno Mitchell

Ernest Beal

Geo Stukes

Jos Hewitt

Jno Kelly

MUSKOKA RIVER

MUSKOKA

MAP OF MONCK TOWNSHIP.

A SCENE ON LAKE ROSSEAU

DEE BANK.

MAP OF WATT TOWNSHIP

CARDWELL

SKELETON LAKE

TROUT LAKE

LAKE ROSSEAU

THREE MILE LAKE

BRANDY LAKE

MONCK

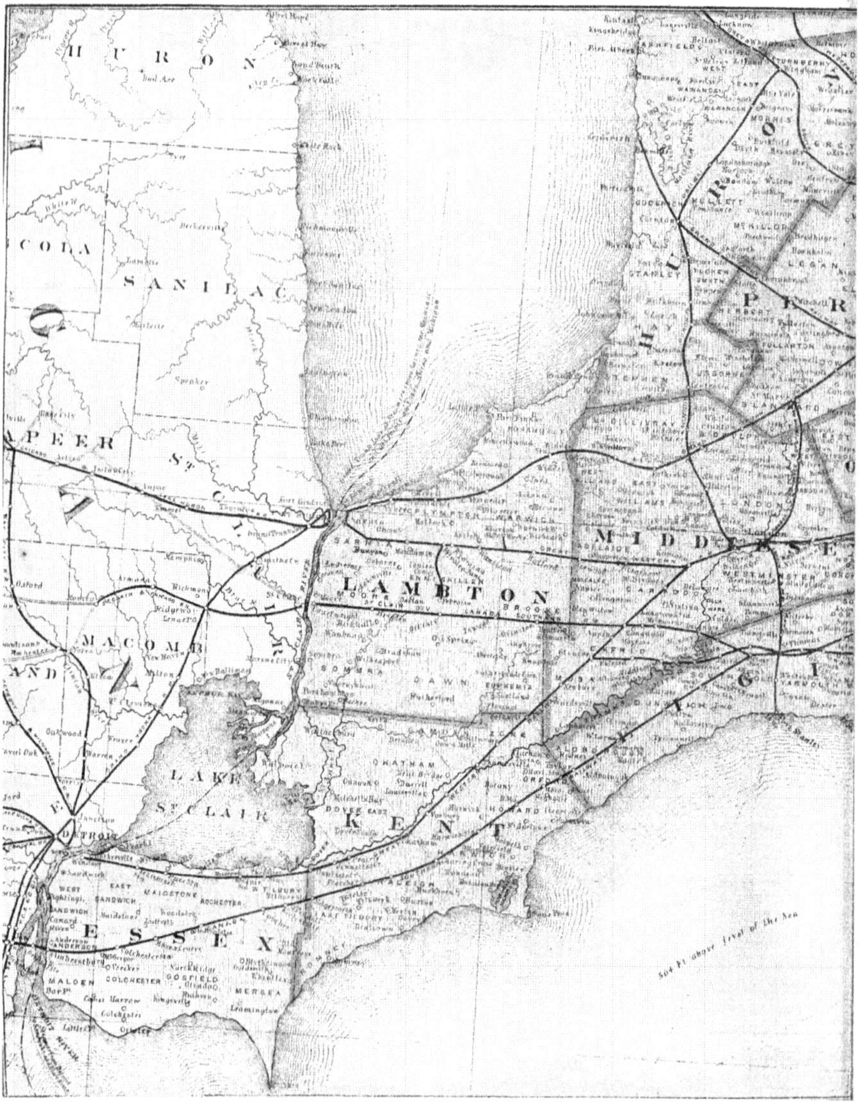

HURON

SANILAC

COLA

LAPEER

ST. CLAIR

MACOMB

LAMBTON

MIDDLE

PER

HURON

LAKE ST. CLAIR

KENT

DETROIT

ESSEX

MALDEN

COLCHESTER

GOSFIELD

MERSEA

Sold by order Trust of This Sea

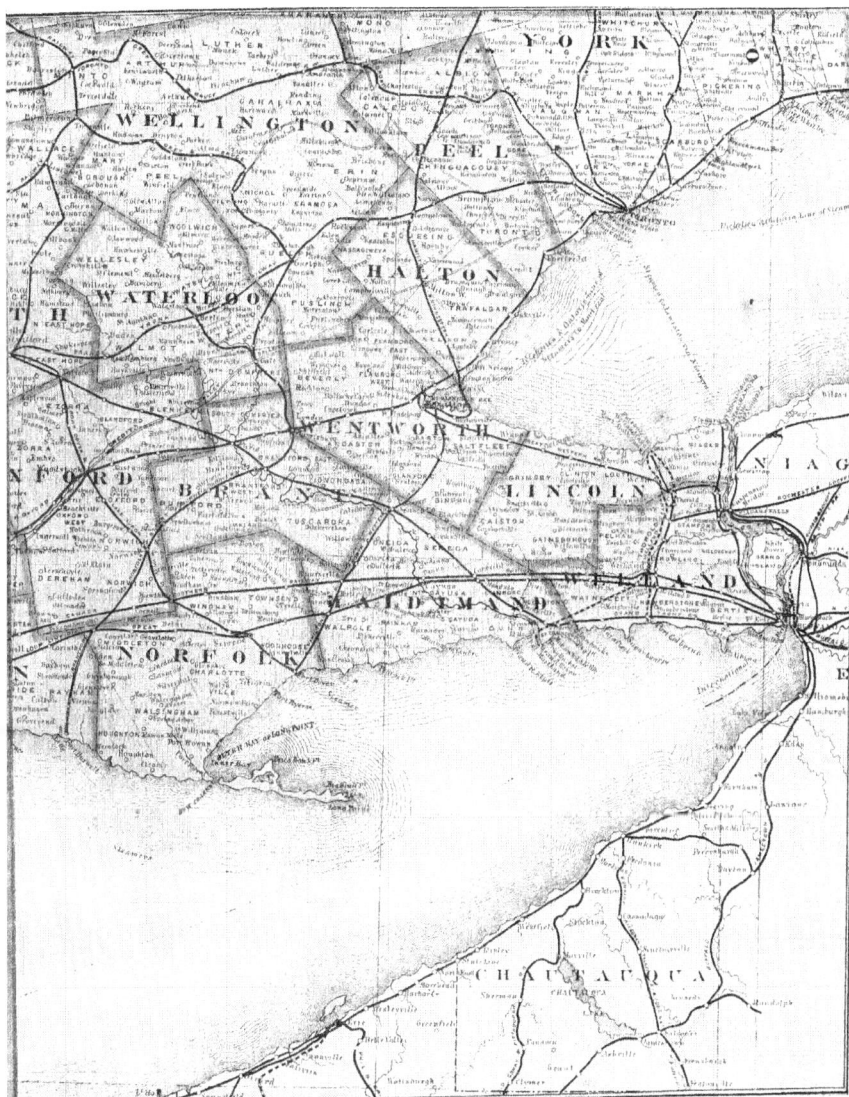

PLAN OF BRACEBRIDGE VILLAGE

Scale 10 Chains per Inch

Drawn by J. Rogers C.E.

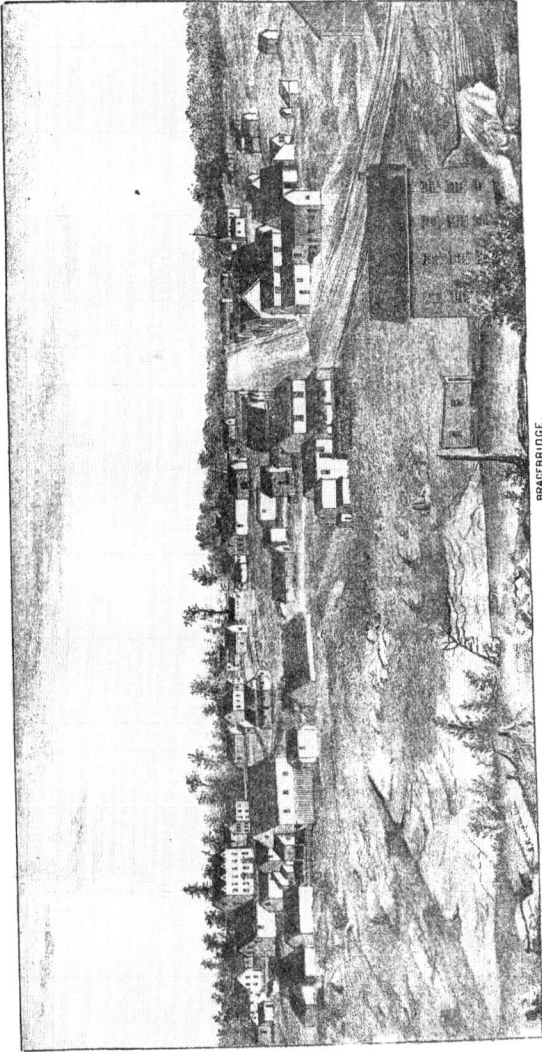

BRACEBRIDGE.

MAP OF MACAULAY TOWNSHIP.

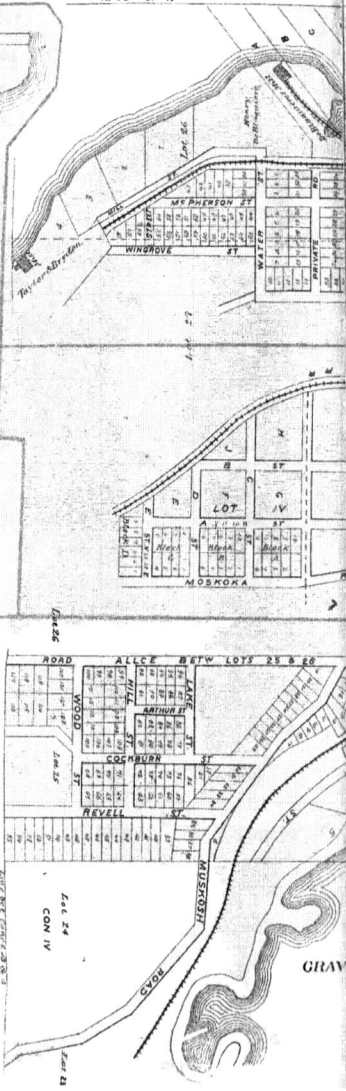

MAP OF **GRAVENHURST** VILLAGE

Scale 10 Chains = 1 inch

WEST GRAVENHURST
Scale 10 Chains per 1 inch

MUSKOKA LAKE

SOUTH BAY

West of Road

BURNETT ST

AUSTIN ST

SARAH ST

MARY ST

JOHN ST

MUSKOKA ST

FIRST ST

SECOND ST

THIRD ST

FOURTH ST

FIFTH ST

SIXTH ST

GULL LAKE

BRACEBRIDGE ROAD

LOT X

MAP OF Mc LEAN TOWNSHIP

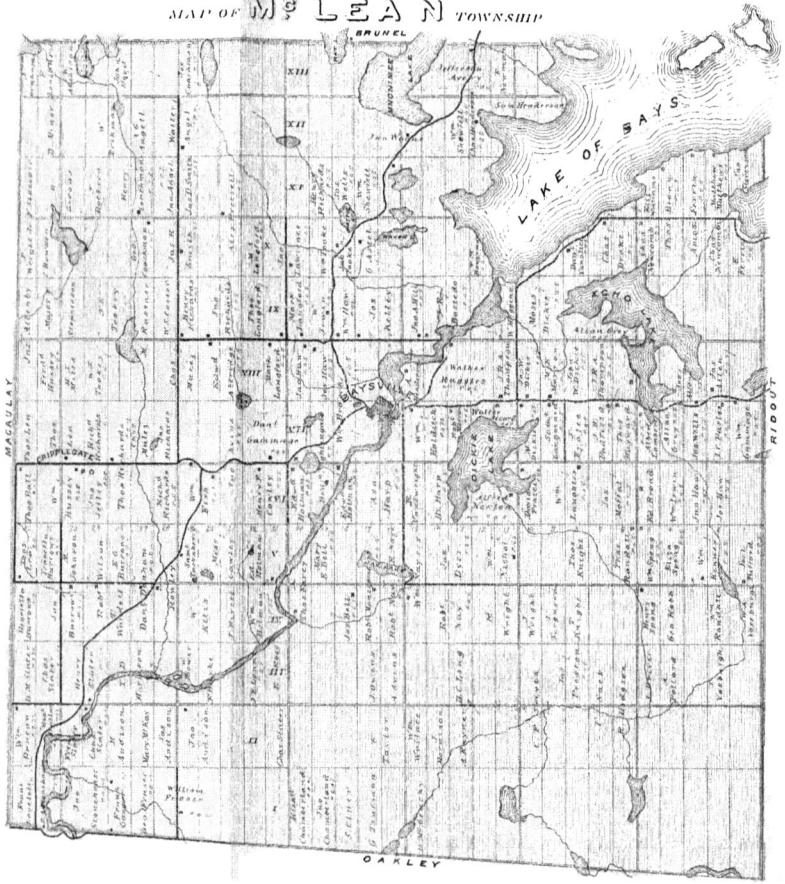

BRUNEL

LAKE OF SAYS

MACAULAY

RIDOUT

BAYSV

ECHO

DICKE

OAKLEY

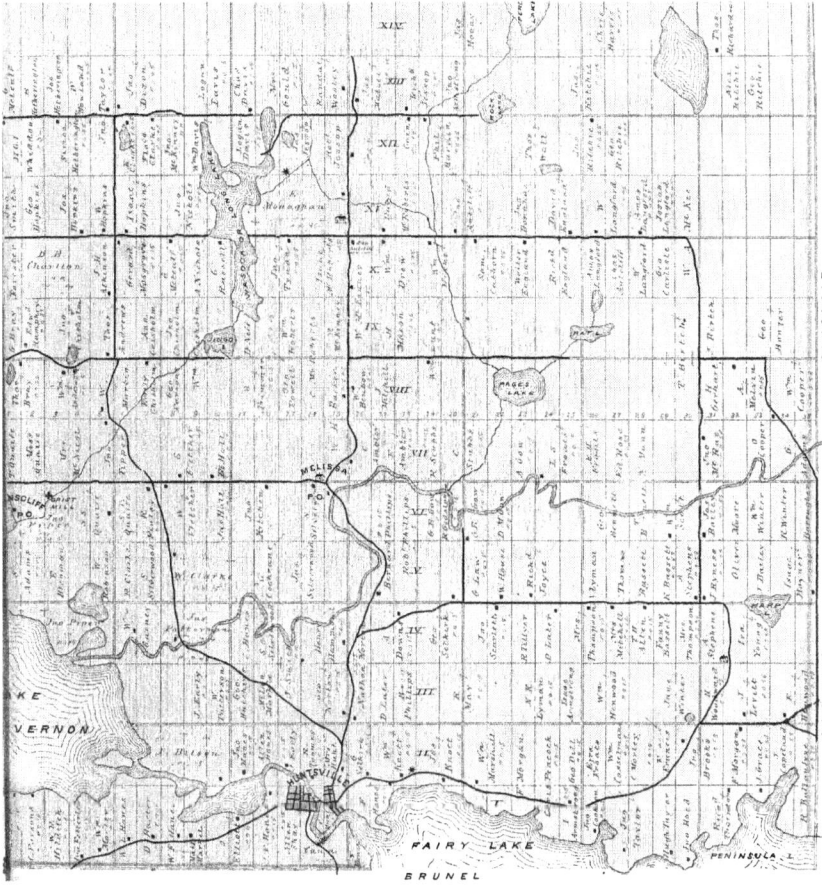

MAP OF BRUNEL TOWNSHIP

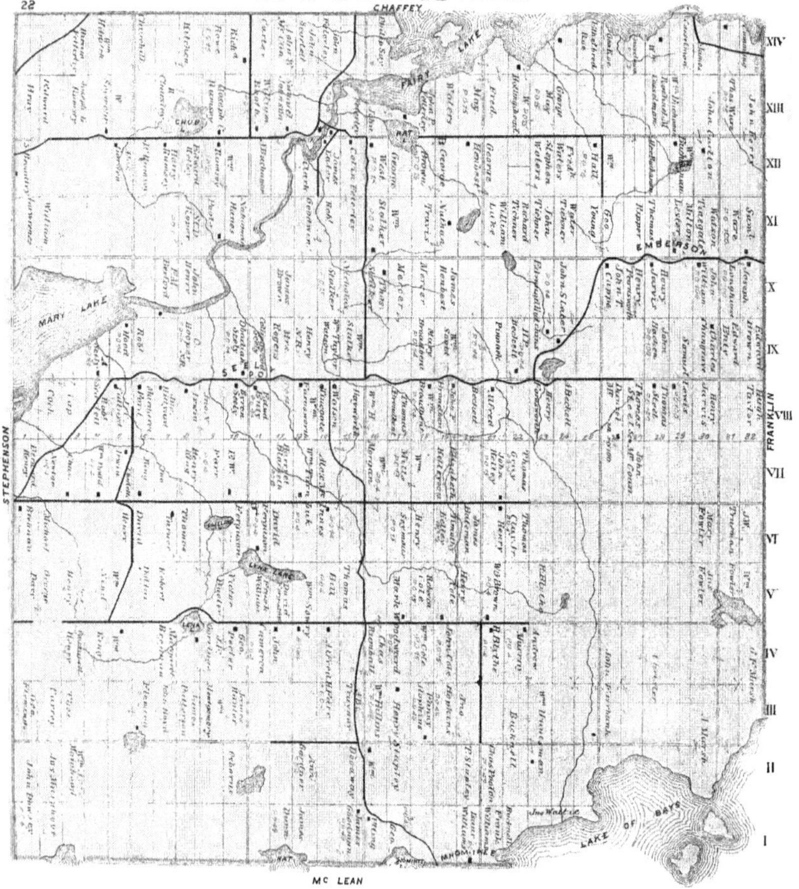

VILLAGE OF PORT SYDNEY, FROM SMITH'S HILL.

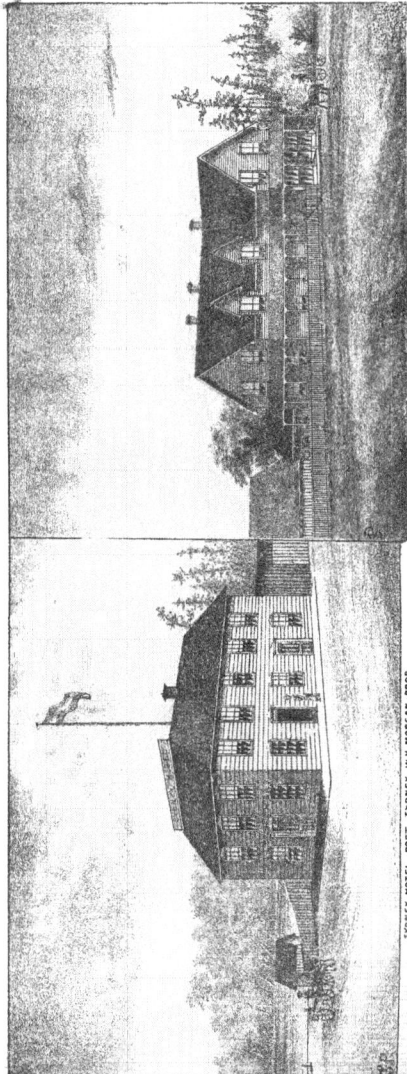

STORE & P.O. PORT SYDNEY, H.C. LABELL, J.P. PROP.

SYDNEY HOTEL, PORT SYDNEY, W.H. MORGAN. PROP

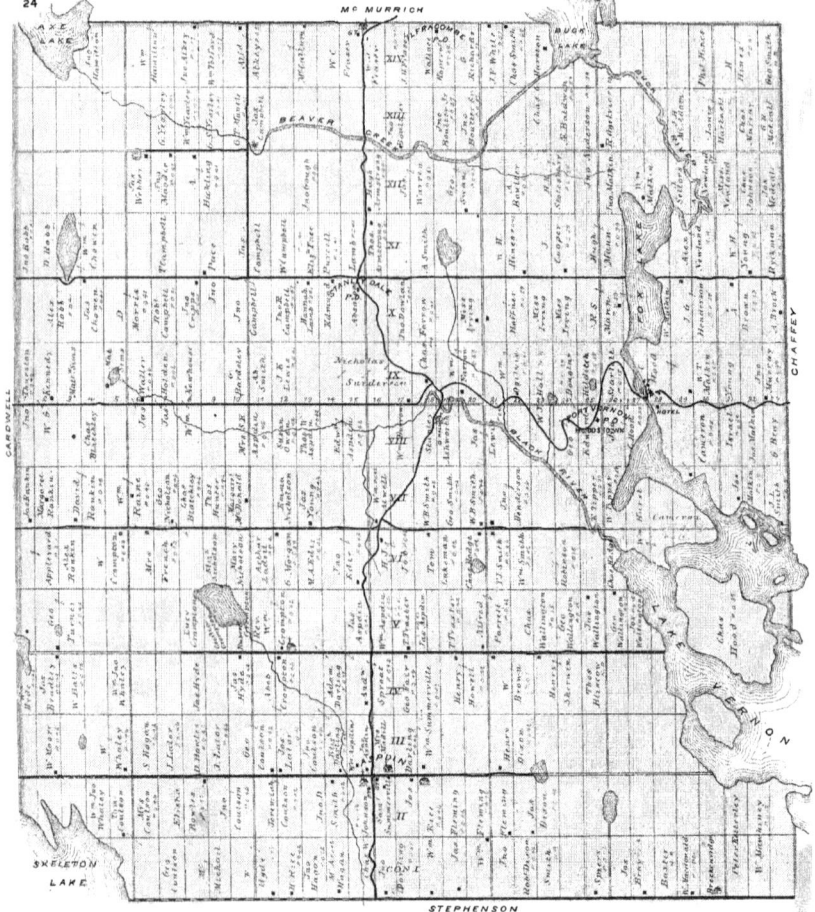

MAP OF **FRANKLIN** TOWNSHIP

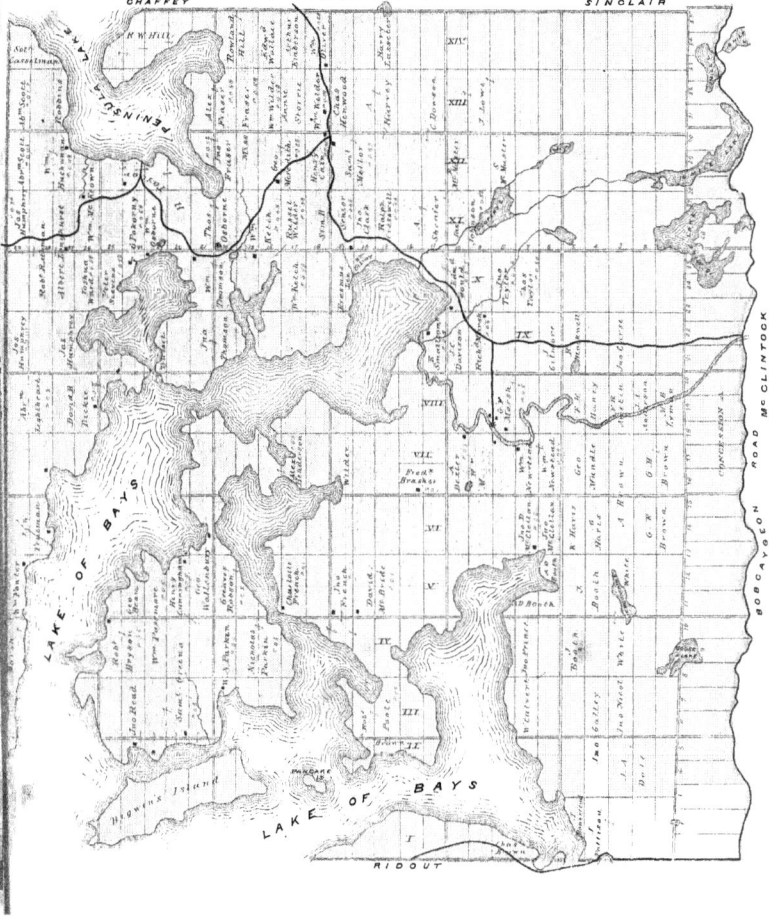

MAP OF **CARDWELL** TOWNSHIP.

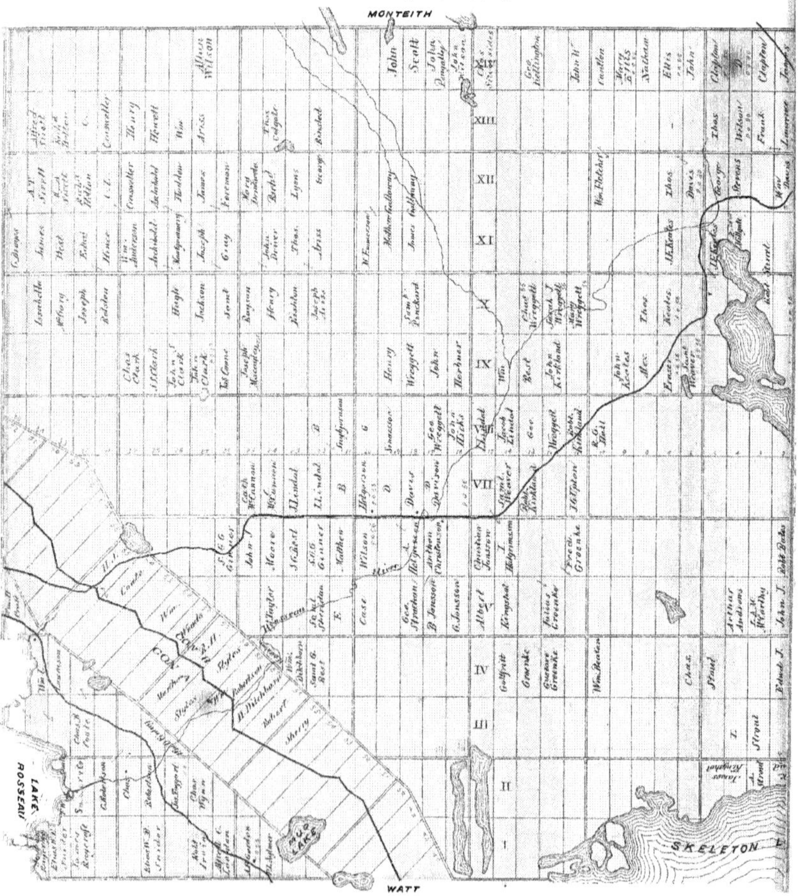

MONTEITH

XIII

XII

XI

X

IX

VIII

VII

VI

V

IV

III

II

I

HUMPHRY

LAKE
ROSSEAU

MUD LAKE

WATT

SKELETON L.

FRANKLIN

TRADING LAKE

TRADING BAY

SHERBORNE ROAD

BOBCAYGEON ROAD

TROUT

ST MARYS LAKE

MARLIN LAKE

SHOE LAKE

GULL LAKE

BLACK RIVER

BLACK LAKE

XIV

XIII

XII

XI

X

IX

VIII

XII

XI

V

IV

III

II

I

HINDON

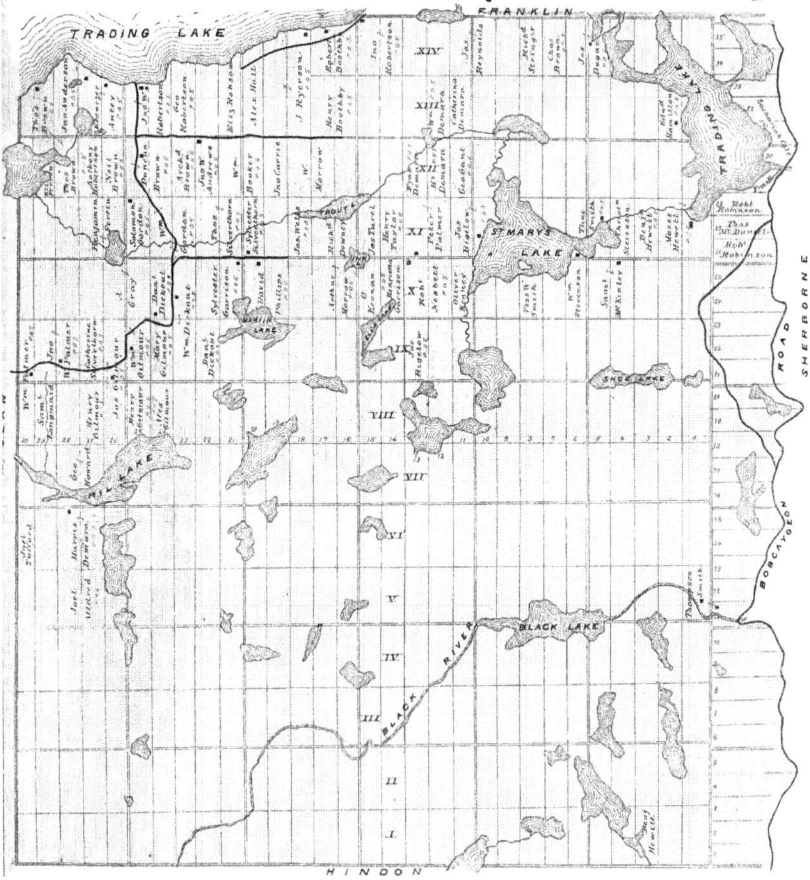

MAP OF **SPENCE** TOWNSHIP

CROFT

MONTEITH

PARRY SOUND
MUSKOKA
NIPISSING
MOWATT
WILSON
FERRIE
LOUNT
MACHAR
ARMOUR
PERRY
RYERSON
McMURRICH
MONTEITH
CHRISTIE
BURTON
HAGERMAN
SPENCE
CHAFFEY
STISTED
BRUNEL
McLEAN
DRAPER
LIVINGSTONE
LAWRENCE
EYRE
CLYDE
NIGHTINGALE
SHERBORNE

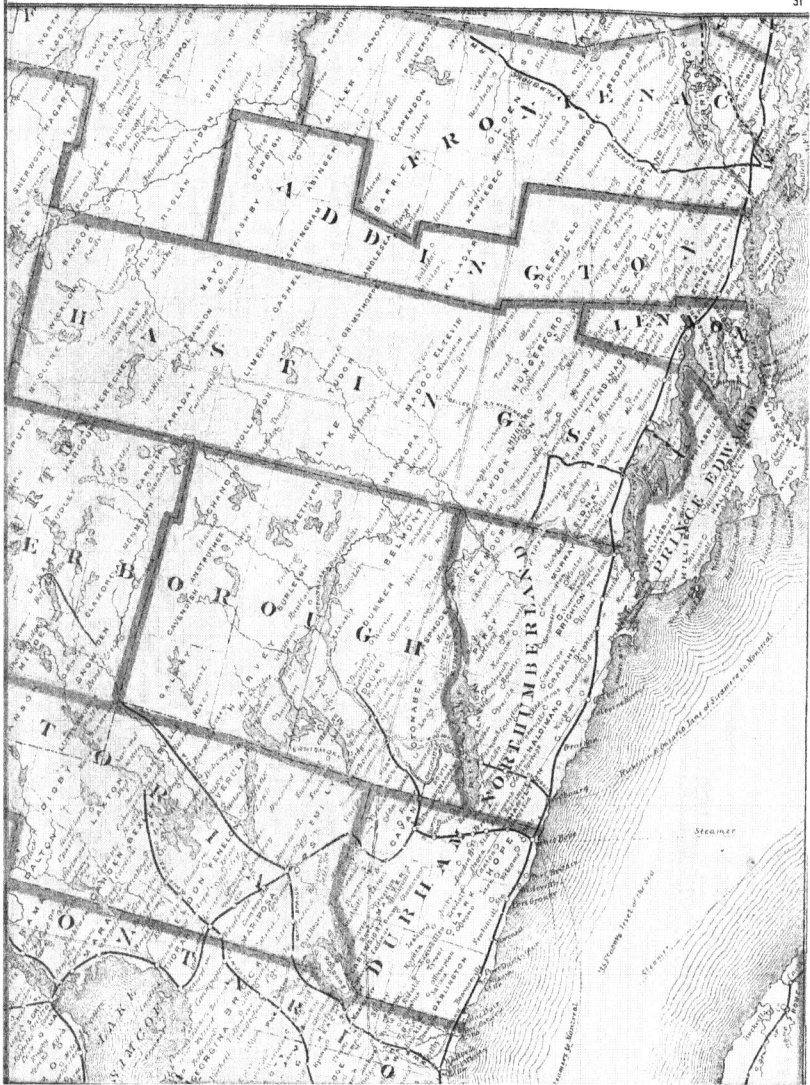

MAP OF **HUMPHREY** TOWNSHIP.

VILLAGE OF
PARRY SOUND
Scale 10 Chains 1 inch.

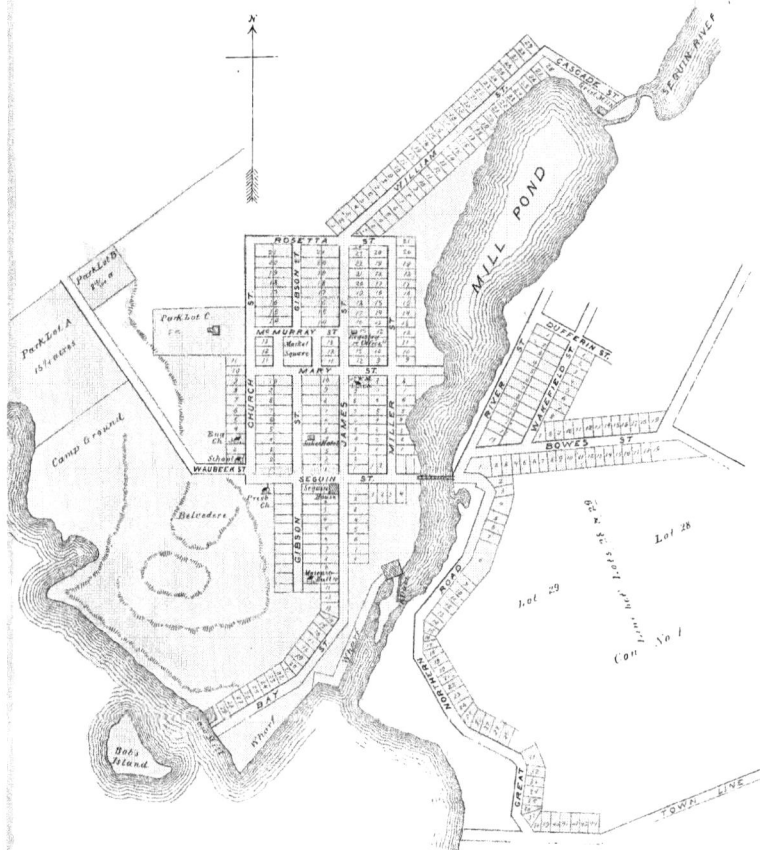

N

ROSETTA ST.

WILLIAM

CASCADE ST.

SEGUIN RIVER

MILL POND

Park Lot B

Park Lot C

Park Lot A

GIBSON ST.

McMURRAY ST.

Market Square

MARY ST.

CHURCH ST.

JAMES ST.

MILLER

RIVER ST.

DUFFERIN ST.

WAKEFIELD

BOWES ST.

Camp Ground

WAUBEEK ST.

SEGUIN ST.
Seguin House

Belvedere

GIBSON ST.

Lot 29

Lot 28

Con her Lots No 29

Con No 1

BAY ST.

Bobs Island

Wharf

GREAT ROAD

ADDISON

TOWN LINE

Lumbermans Dam . Near . McKellar

MAP OF MᶜDOUGALL TOWNSHIP.

BELOW LORIMER LAKE.

Lumbermans Dam . Near . McKellar

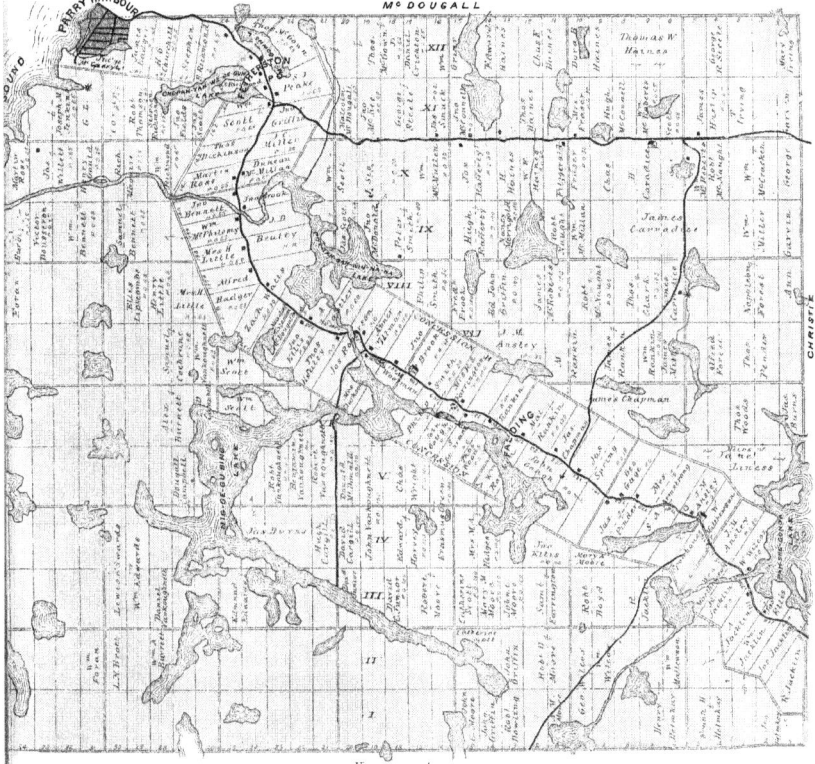

MAP OF FOLEY TOWNSHIP

McDOUGALL

PARRY HARBOUR

CHRISTIE

Unsurveyed

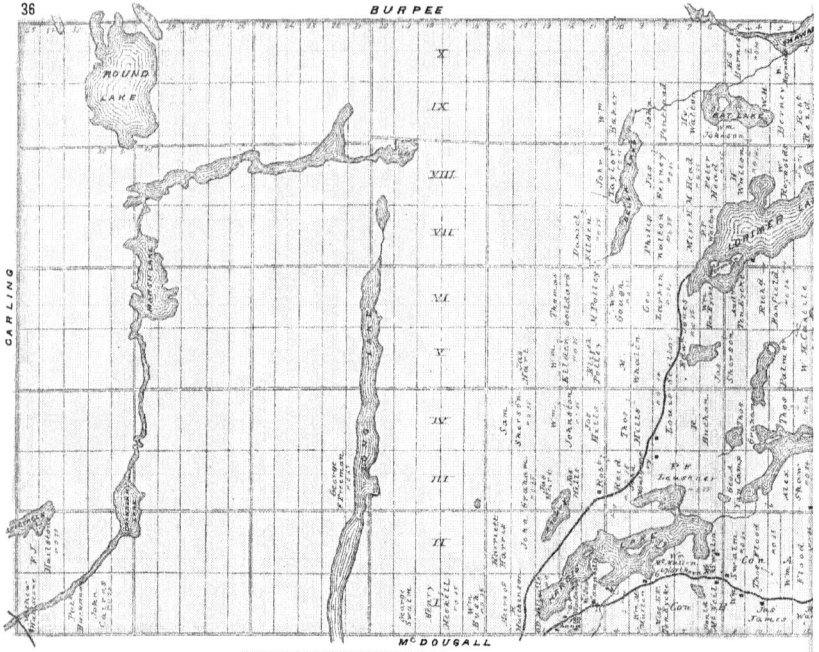

MAP OF MᶜKELLAR VILLAGE
Scale 600 Feet - 1 inch

PARRY. HARBOUR.

SHANTY, ON THE MAGANETAWAN RIVER.

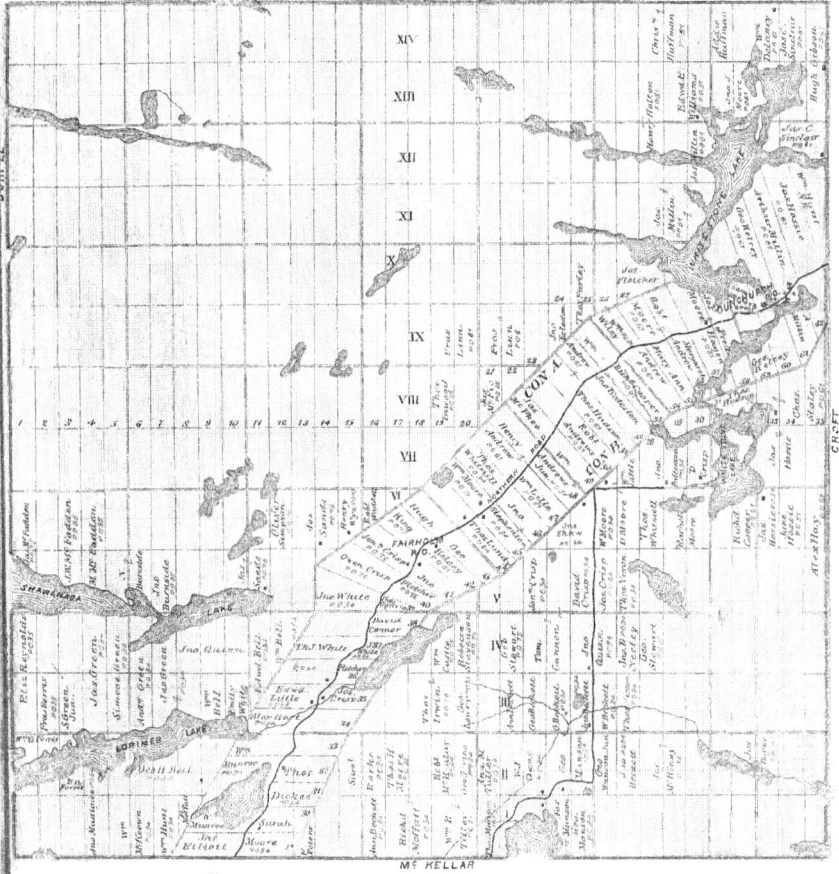

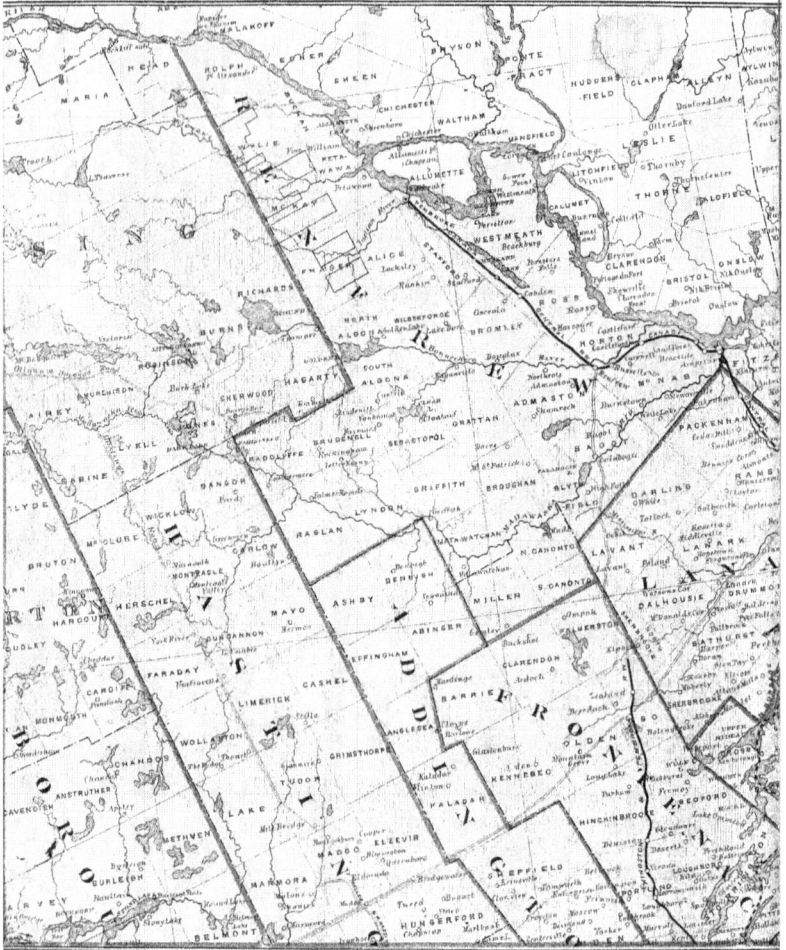

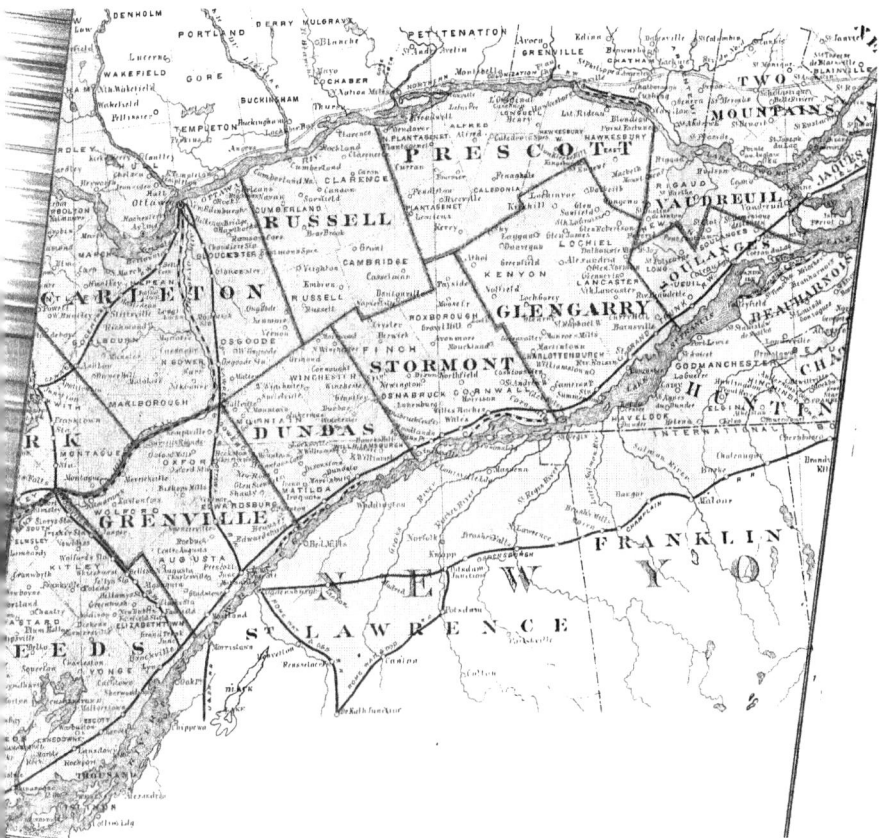

MAP OF McKELLAR TOWNSHIP.

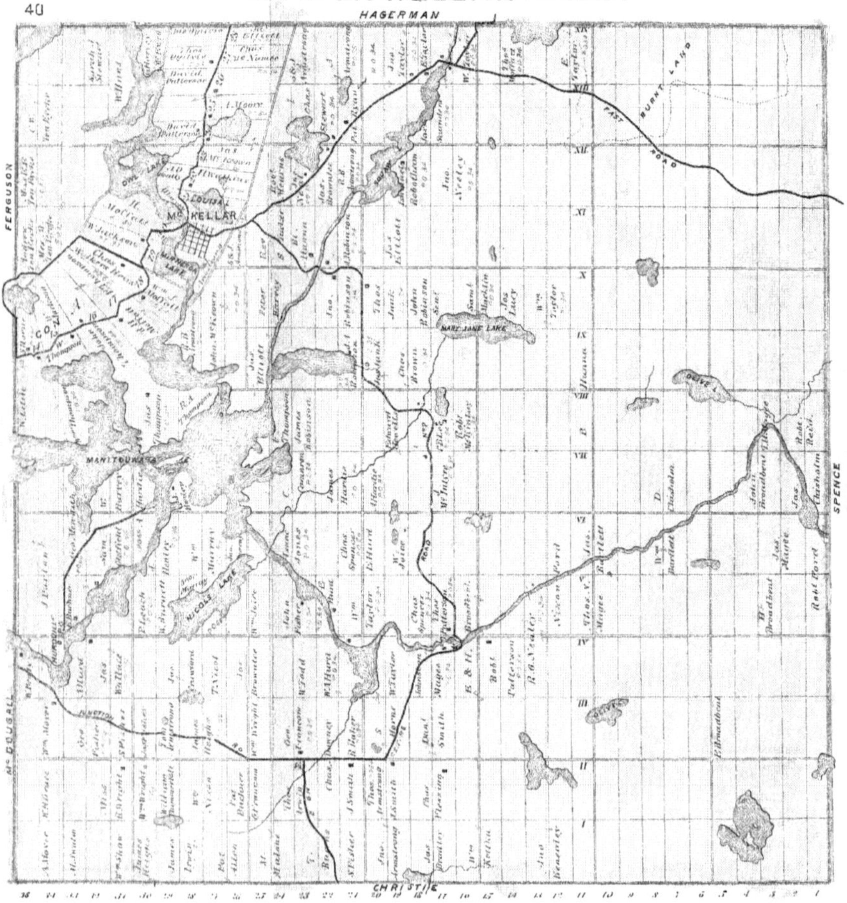

HAGERMAN
FERGUSON
SPENCE
CHRISTIE
McDOUGALL
OWL LAKE
McKELLAR
MANITOUWABA LAKE
MARY JANE LAKE
OLIVE L.
NICOLS LAKE
EAST BURNT LAND ROAD

JAS WALKER'S GENERAL STORE.

RES OF JOHN ARMSTRONG ESQ. MᶜKELLAR.

STORE & POST OFFICE. MᶜKELLAR. B.&J. ARMSTRONG, PROPS.

MᶜKELLAR HOUSE. W.F.THOMSON PROPᴿ

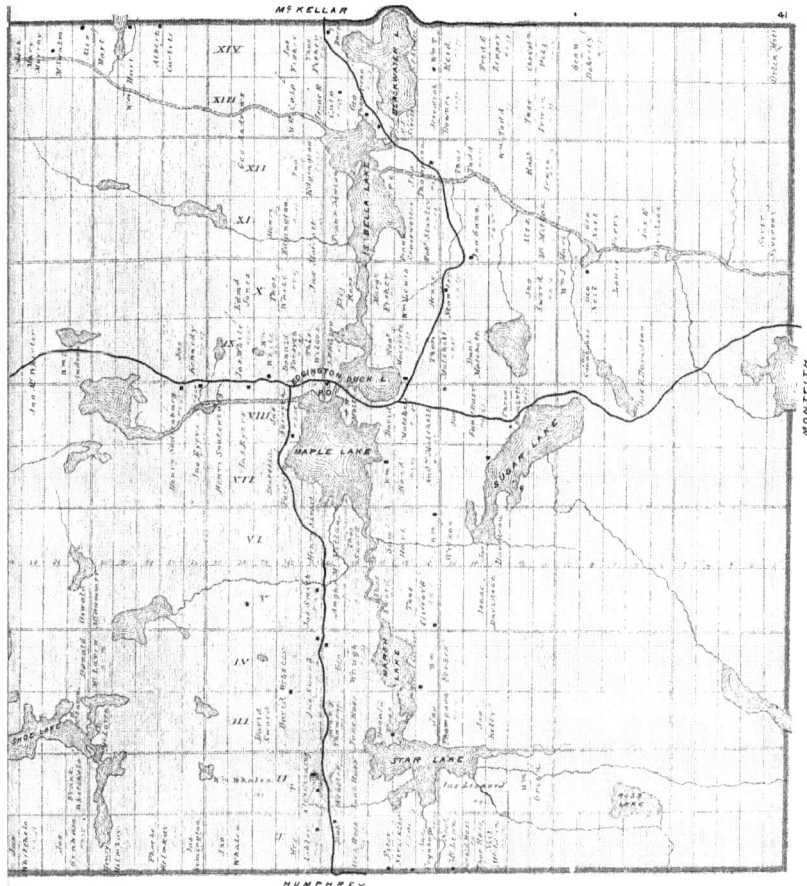

MAP OF **ROSSEAU** VILLAGE
HELMSLEY .
Scale 10 chs = 1 inch

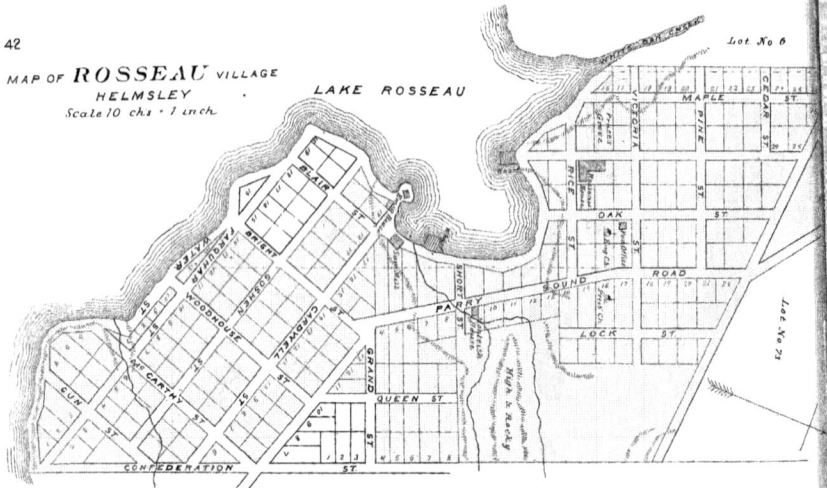

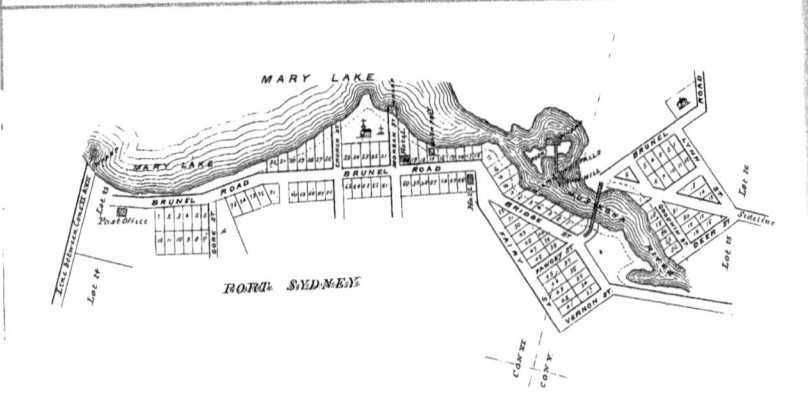

LAKE ROSSEAU

Lot No 6

CEDAR ST.

MAPLE ST.

PINE ST.

VIRGINIA ST.

RICE ST.

OAK ST.

ROAD

LOCK ST.

Lot No 7a

BLAIR

WALTER

SYDENHAM

BRENT

WOODHOUSE

JOSEPH

CROMWELL

McCARTHY

GUN ST.

GRAND ST.

QUEEN ST.

PARRY SOUND

SHORT ST.

High & Rocky

CONFEDERATION ST.

MARY LAKE

WHITE OAK ROAD

MARY LAKE

BRUNEL ROAD

BRUNEL ROAD

Post Office

Line Provincial Road

Post Office

PORT SYDNEY

Lot 15

Sideline

Lot 14

CON XI

AKO3

SPENGE..

XIV

XIII

XII

XI

X

IX

VIII

VII

VI

V

IV

III

II

I

SEGUIN FALLS

Sutton Co.

DRY

HOTEL

CARDWELL

Mc MURRICH

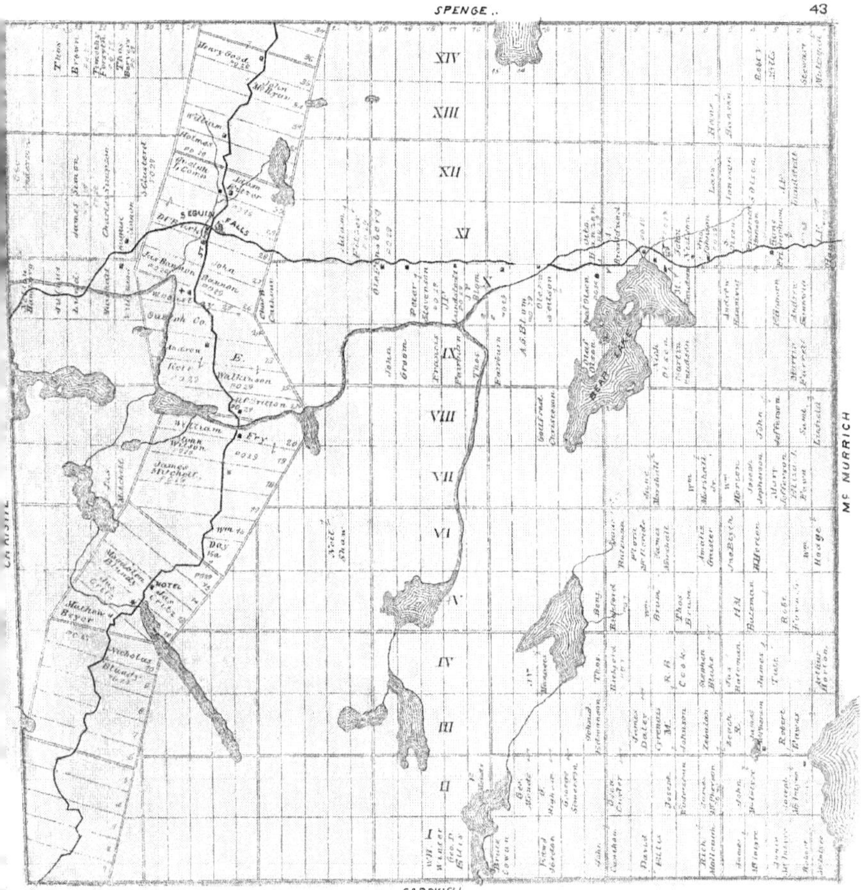

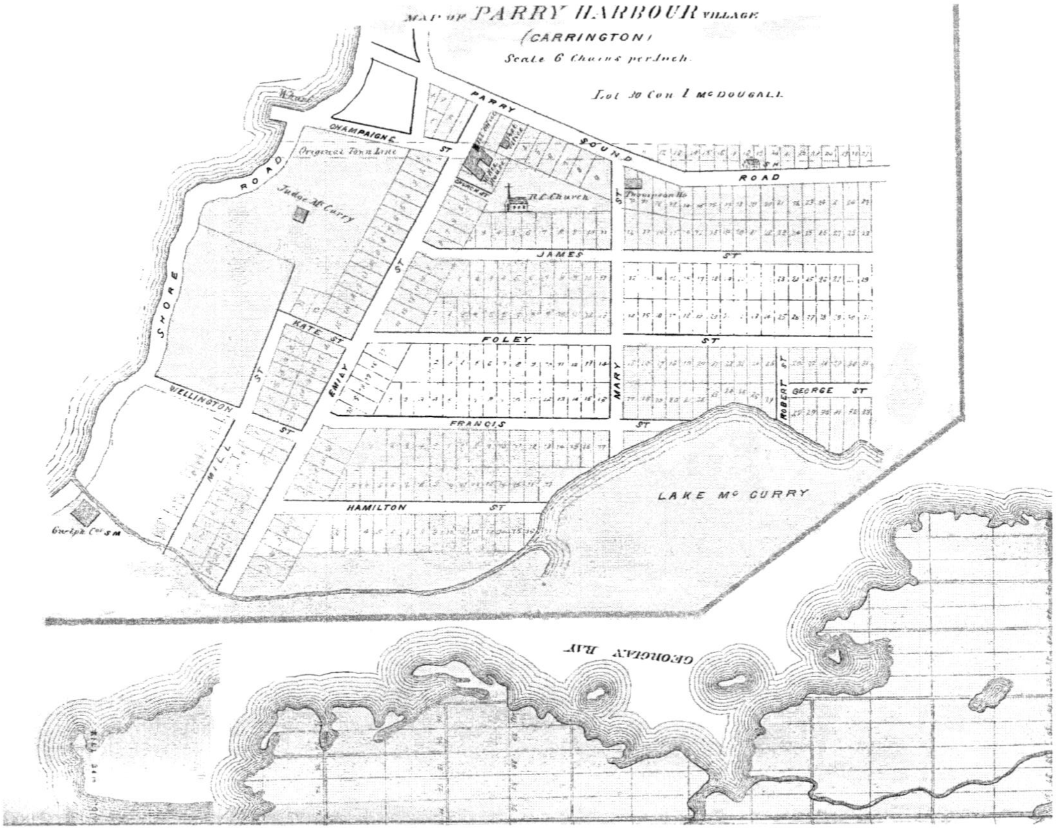

MAP OF PARRY HARBOUR VILLAGE
(CARRINGTON)
Scale 6 Chains per Inch.
Lot 30 Con 1 McDOUGALL
PARRY SOUND ROAD
CHAMPAIGNE ST
Original Town Line
SHORE ROAD
Judge McCurry
R.C. Church
JAMES ST
FOLEY ST
FRANCIS ST
HAMILTON ST
KATE ST
EMILY ST
MARY ST
ROBERT ST
GEORGE ST
WELLINGTON ST
MILL ST
LAKE McCURRY
Guelph Co's SM
GEORGIAN BAY

SHAWANAGA

CHE PA RONGE RIVER

X

IX

VIII

VII

VI

V

IV

III

II

I

XII

XI

X

IX

VIII

VII

FERGUSON

McDOUGALL

PARRY SOUND

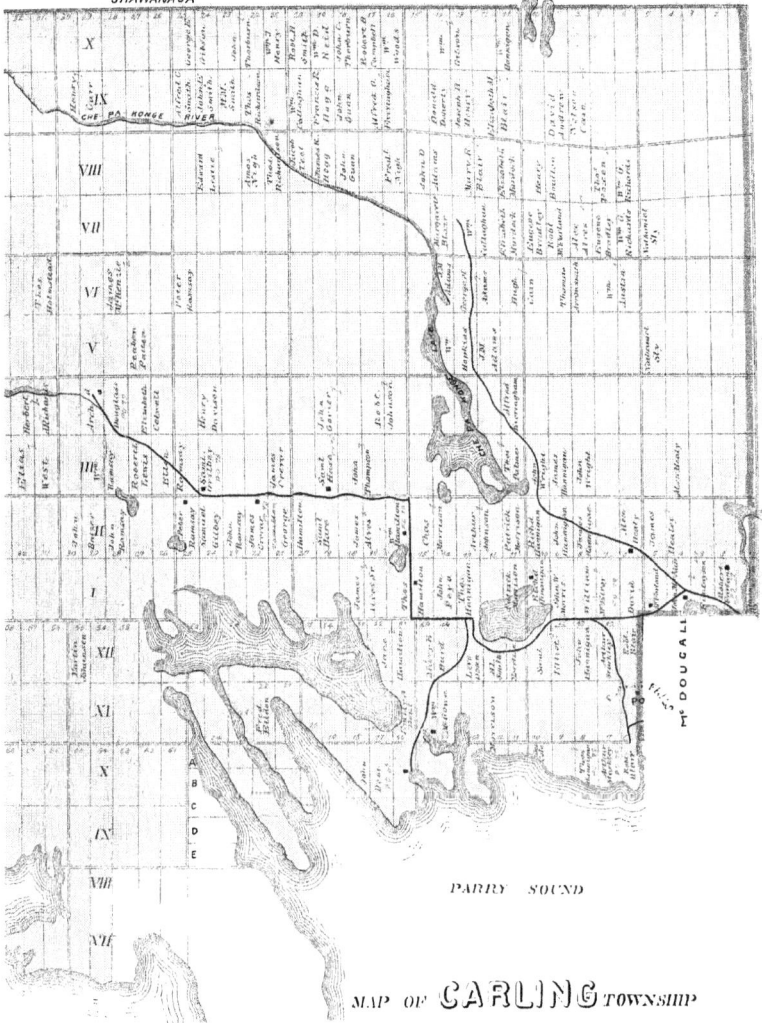

MAP OF CARLING TOWNSHIP

MAP OF McMURRICH TOWNSHIP.

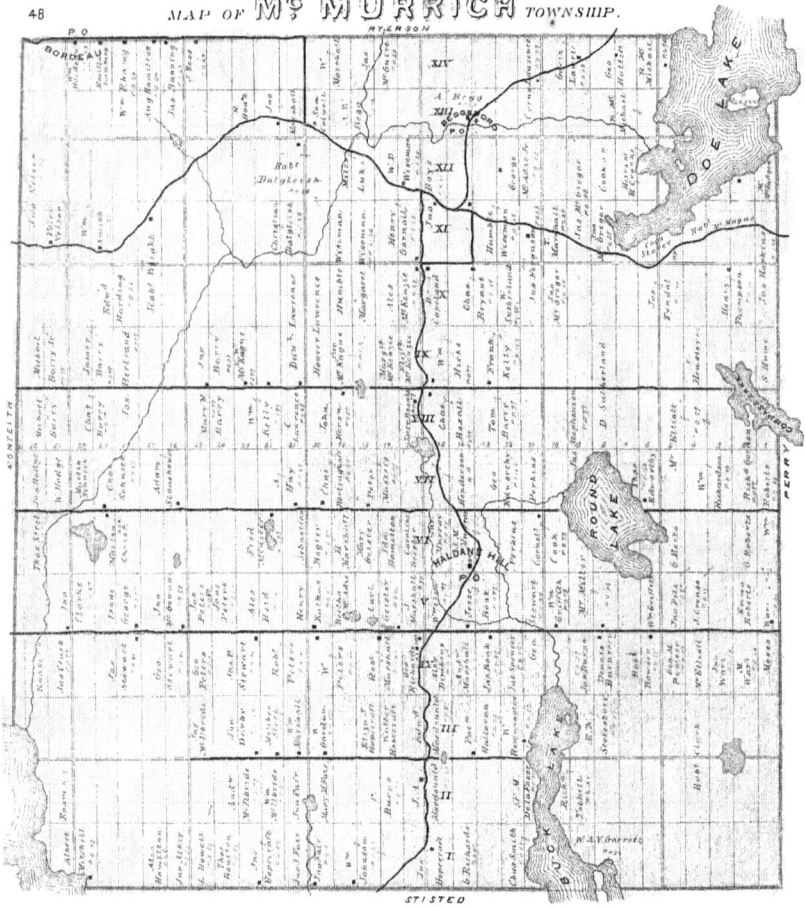

RYERSON

XIV

DOE LAKE

BORDEAU
P.O.

XIII
SPRUCEDALE
P.O.

XII

XI

X

IX

VIII

VII

PENINSULA

VI

HALDANE HILL

ROUND LAKE

V

PERRY

IV

III

II

I

BUCK LAKE

ST STED

MAGARETAWAN.

M°KELLAR.

MAP OF CHAPMAN TOWNSHIP

LOUNT
RYERSON
STRONG
CHELMSFORD P.O.
CLAVERTON P.O.
MAGANETAWAN
XIV
XIII
XII
XI
X
IX
VIII
VII
VI
V
IV
III
II
I
HORN LAKE
LOCK

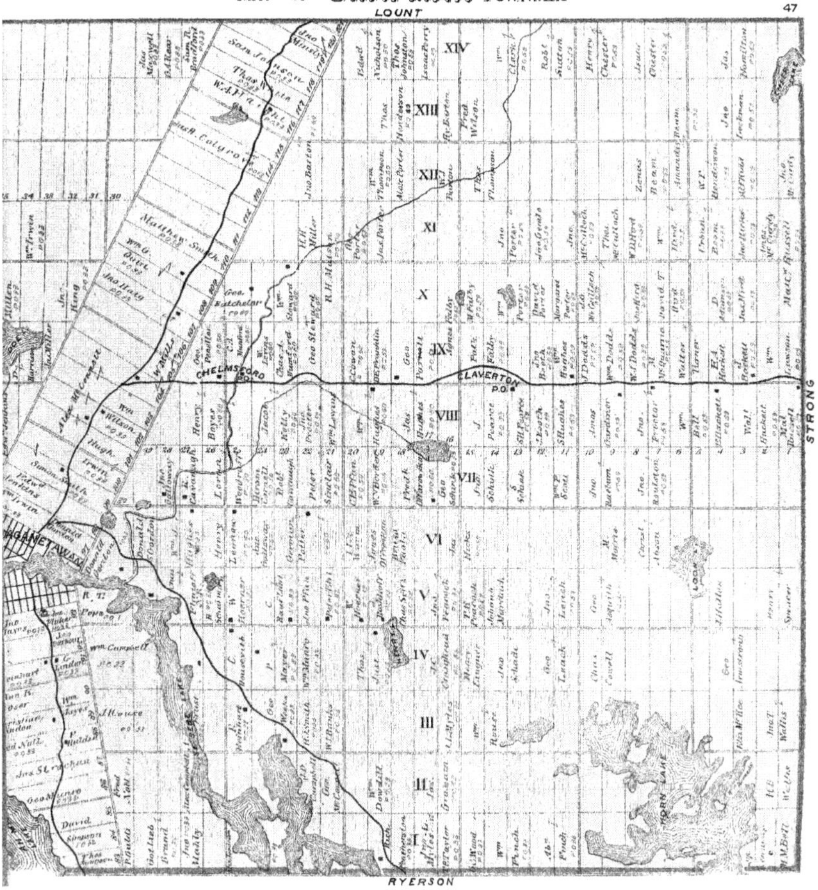

MAP OF CROFT TOWNSHIP.

FERRIE

SPENCE

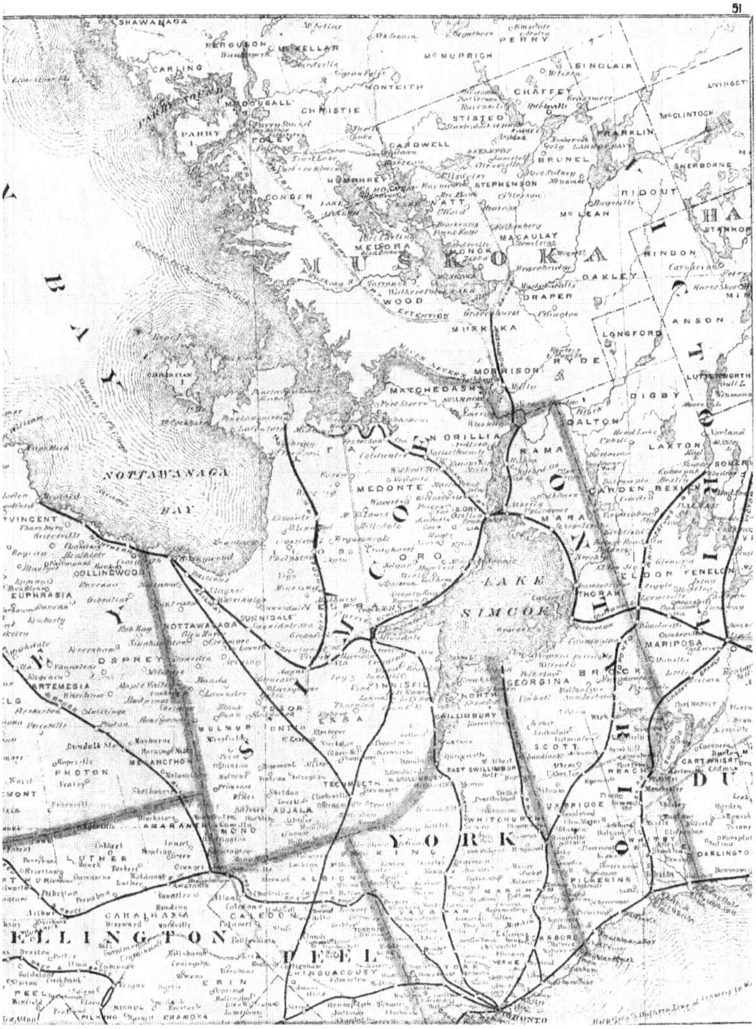
SHAWANAGA
FERGUSON
McKELLAR
PERRY
McMURRICH
SINCLAIR
CARLING
MONTEITH
CHAFFEY
McDOUGALL
CHRISTIE
STISTED
FRANKLIN
McCLINTOCK
FOLEY
CARDWELL
BRUNEL
SHERBORNE
HUMPHREY
STEPHENSON
CONGER
WATT
RIDOUT
McLEAN
MEDORA
MACAULAY
MUSKOKA
RINDON
OAKLEY
WOOD
DRAPER
ANSON
LONGFORD
RYDE
MORRISON
MATCHEDASH
DIGBY
DALTON
N. ORILLIA
RAMA
LAXTON
NOTTAWASAGA
BAY
MEDONTE
CARDEN
BEXLEY
MARA
COLLINGWOOD
EUPHRASIA
LAKE
SIMCOE
THORAH
ELDON
FENELON
SUNNIDALE
NOTTAWASAGA
OSPREY
MARIPOSA
ARTEMESIA
INNISFIL
GEORGINA
BROCK
MULMUR
ESSA
TOSSORONTIO
NORTH GWILLIMBURY
SCOTT
MELANCTHON
PROTON
TECUMSETH
EAST GWILLIMBURY
REACH
CARTWRIGHT
ADJALA
WHITCHURCH
UXBRIDGE
AMARANTH
MONO
YORK
KING
WHITBY
DARLINGTON
LUTHER
ALBION
MARKHAM
PICKERING
CALEDON
VAUGHAN
WELLINGTON
PEEL
SCARBORO
CHINGUACOUSY
ERIN
ERAMOSA
NICHOL
TORONTO
SIMCOE
ONTARIO
VICTORIA
DU

MAP OF **ARMOUR** TOWNSHIP.

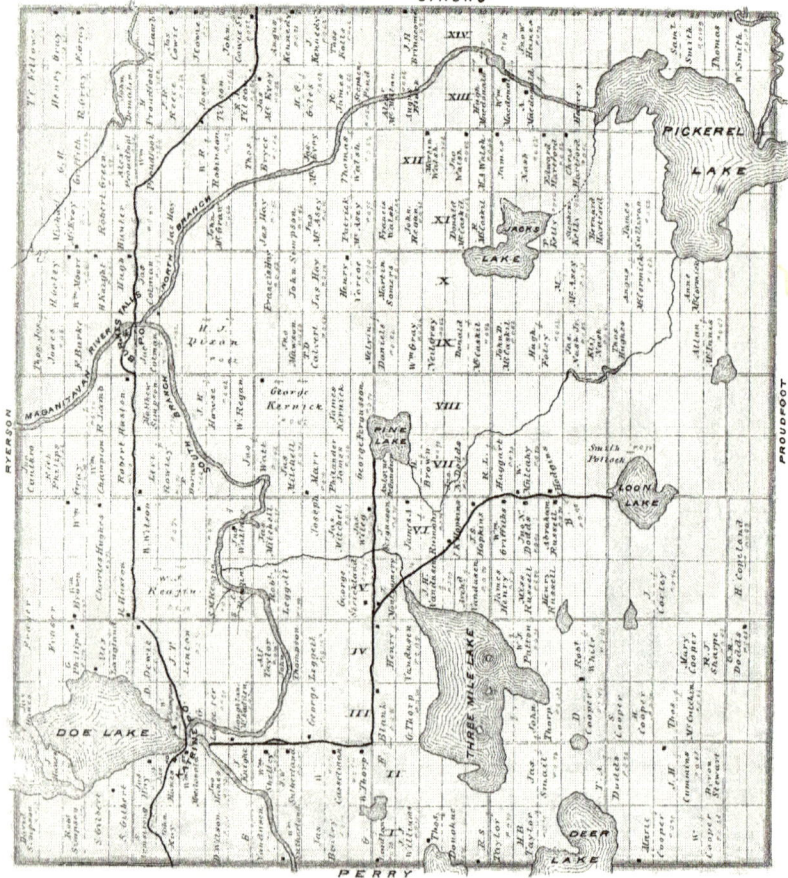

MAP OF STRONG TOWNSHIP.

MACHAR

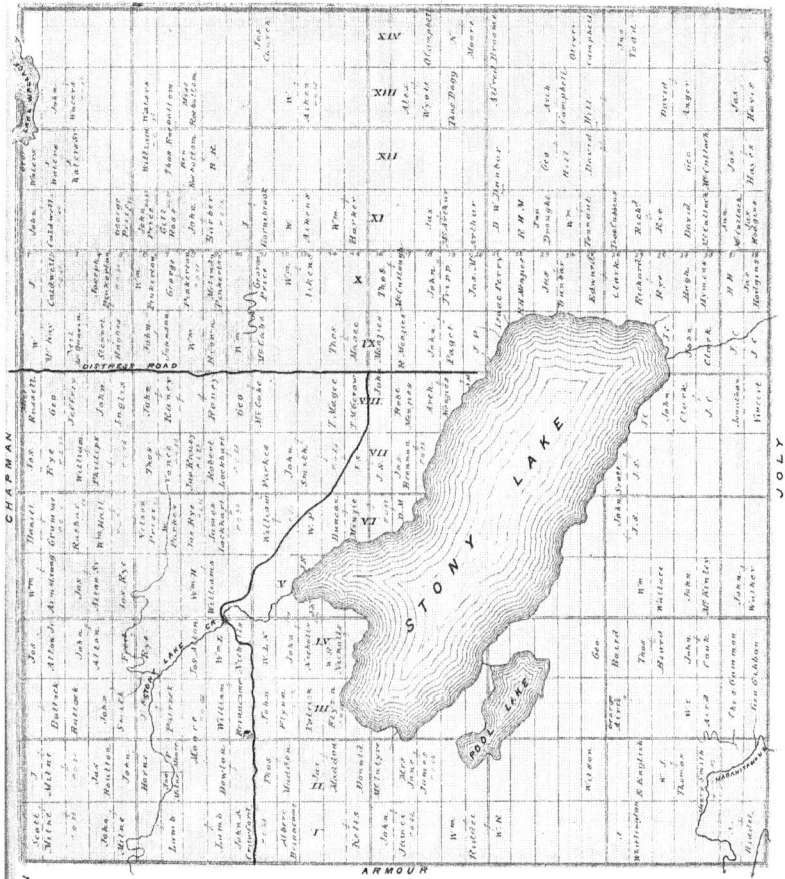

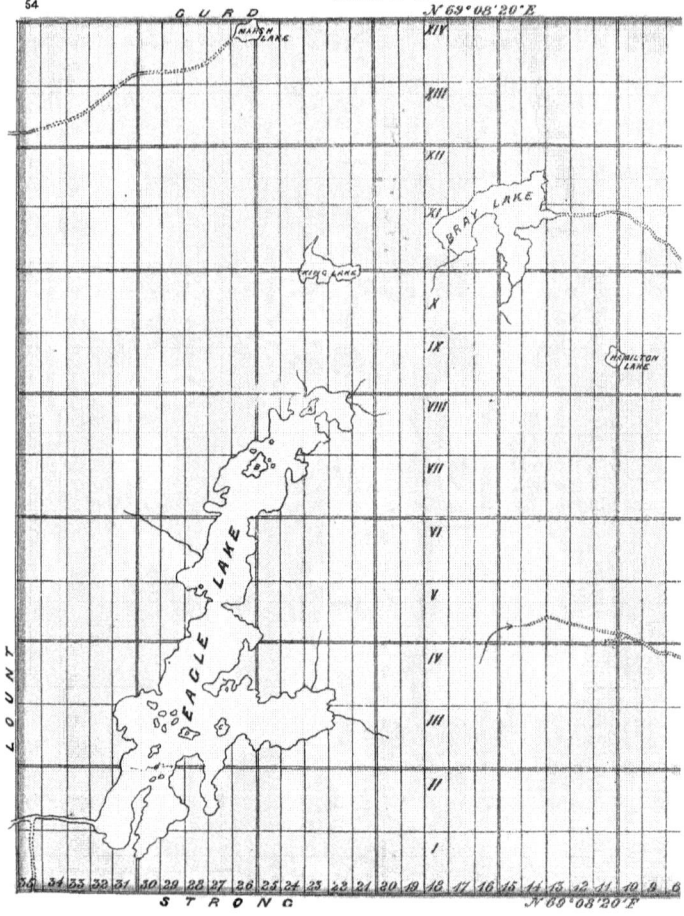

MAP OF **MACHAR** TOWNSHIP

GURD

N 69° 08' 20" E

MARSH LAKE

XIV

XIII

XII

XI

BRAY LAKE

TIRG LAKE

X

IX

HAMILTON LAKE

VIII

VII

EAGLE LAKE

VI

V

IV

III

II

I

LOUNT

36 34 35 32 31 30 29 28 27 26 25 24 23 22 21 20 19 18 17 16 15 14 13 12 11 10 9 8

STRONG

N 69° 08' 20" E

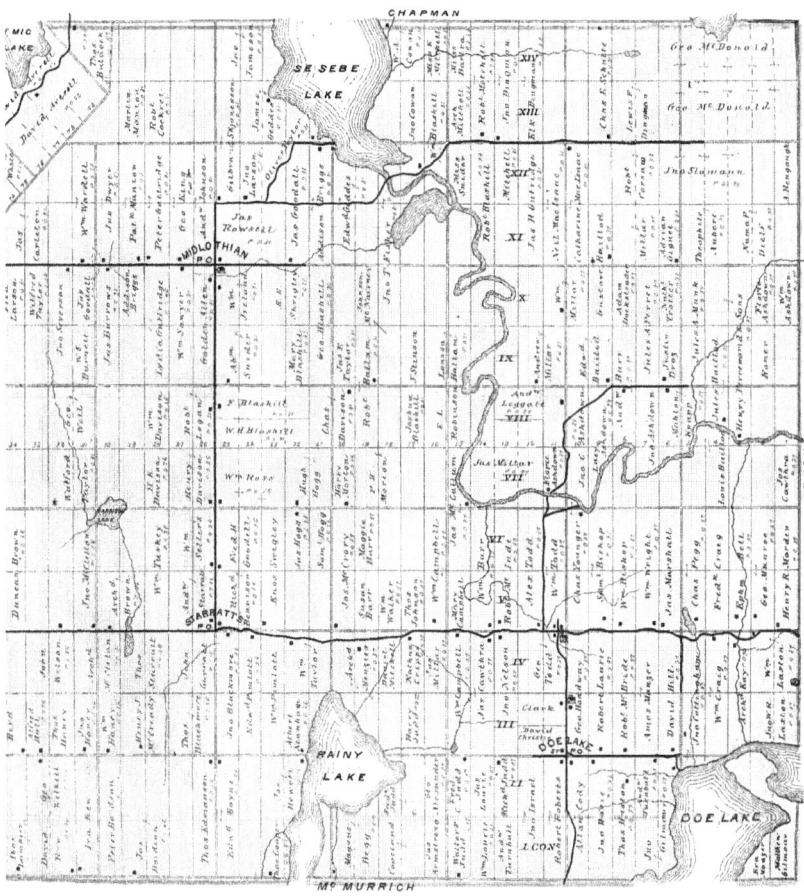

MAP OF
NIPISSING
TOWNSHIP

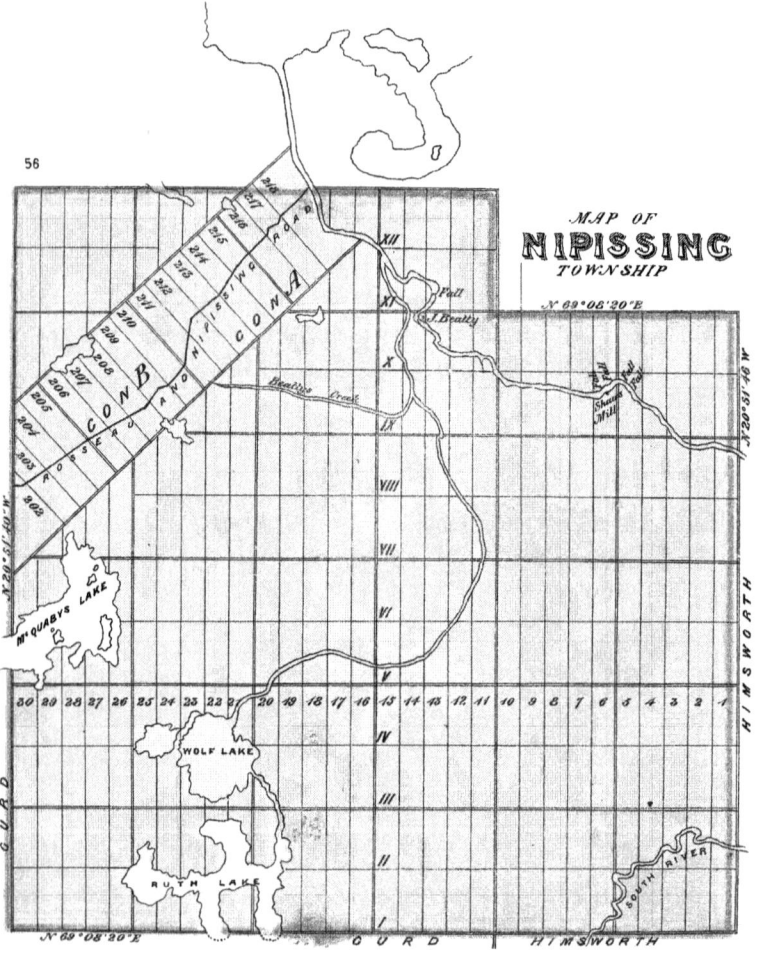

N 69°08'20"E

CON A

CON B

NIPISSING ROAD

ROSEBERRY ROAD

N 20°51'40"W

N 20°51'46"W

301
302
303
304
305
306
307
208
209
210
211
212
213
214
215
216
217
218

XII
XI
X
IX
VIII
VII
VI
V
IV
III
II

Fall

C.J.Brealty

Grist & Saw
Shingle
Mill

Healtice Creek

M^c QUABYS LAKE

WOLF LAKE

RUTH LAKE

SOUTH RIVER

HIMSWORTH

GURD

30 29 28 27 26 25 24 23 22 21 20 19 18 17 16 15 14 13 12 11 10 9 8 7 6 5 4 3 2 1

N 69°08'20"E

GURD   HIMSWORTH

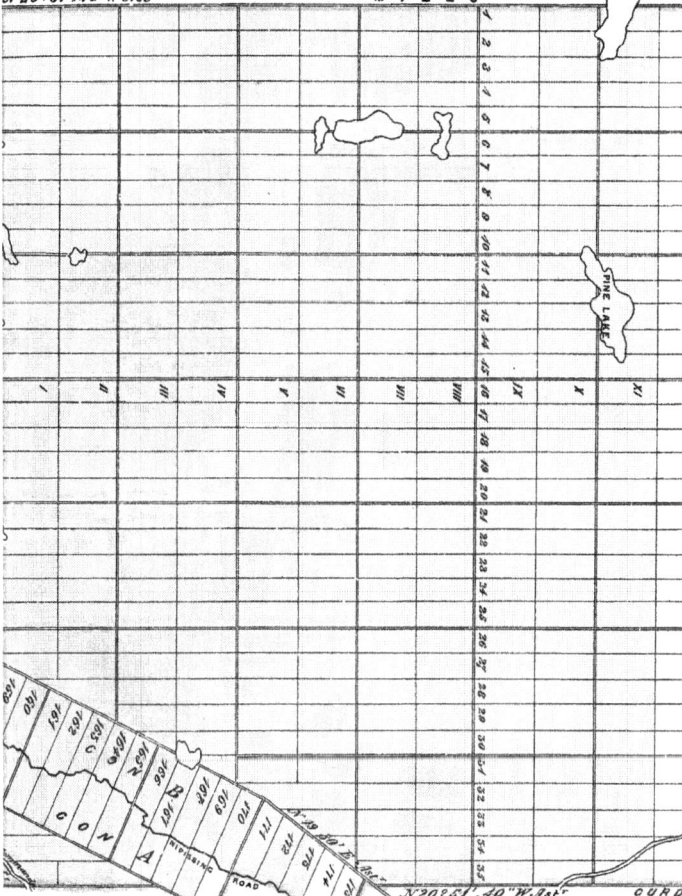

MAP OF **PRINGLE** TOWNSHIP

MAP OF **HIMSWORTH** TOWNSHIP

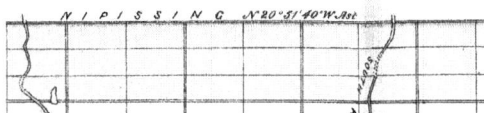

N I P I S S I N G   N.20°51'40'W.Ast

MAP OF BETHUNE TOWNSHIP

PROUDFOOT N.69°08'26

CASHMAN BROTHERS & CO.

Keep the largest and best selected stock of

Groceries, Dry Goods, Ready-Made Clothing, Boots and Shoes in the District.

Hunting and Fishing Parties will find it advantageous to buy their supplies from them.

AGRICULTURAL HALL, - - - - MANITOBA STREET.

DANIELS & MAY,

BRACEBRIDGE AND HUNTSVILLE.

WHOLESALE AND RETAIL DEALERS IN SHELF AND HEAVY HARDWARE,

Cook, Box, Parlor and Patent Heating Stoves, Bar Iron and Steel Nails, Locks and Hinges, Putty, Glass, Scythes, Forks, Shovels, Spades, Axes, Adzes and Edge Tools of all kinds, Guns, Revolvers, &c., Ammunition of every description, Paints, Oils, Varnish and Brushes, Sewing Machines, Ploughs, Fanning Mills, Cutting Boxes, Horse Powers and Implements of all kinds. None but first-class tinsmiths employed. Eave Troughing a specialty.
Daniels & May buy for cash and sell for a marginal profit.

JOSEPH COOPER,

Saw and Shingle Mill,

RIVER STREET, BRACEBRIDGE.

Well Seasoned Lumber Always on Hand.

Orders for Bill Staff promptly attended to. Desirable Village Lots for sale at moderate prices.

MUSKOKA CARRIAGE WORKS

JOHN HAW,

Manufacturer of

Waggons, Buggies, Sleighs,

CUTTERS, &c., &c.

REPAIRING NEATLY EXECUTED.

Horse-shoeing done with neatness and dispatch.

BLACKSMITH'S SHOP,

Ontario Street,

STEPHEN JARRETT, Prop.

All Kinds of Smith's Work

Executed promptly and satisfactorily.

CHARGES MODERATE.

BRITISH ENSIGN.

W. O. TURNER,

Respectfully announces to the public that he has opened out his new store, opposite the Queen's Hotel, with a most complete stock of Dry Goods, Millinery, Groceries, which he is selling at bottom prices.

THE MUSKOKA HERALD,

A Liberal-Conservative Journal, devoted to literature, politics, local and general news, household and agricultural affairs, &c., is published at The "Herald" Printing Office, Orange Hall Building, Manitoba Street, every Thursday morning, and will be sent to any address, postage pre-paid by the publishers, on receipt of the subscription, $1.25, strictly in advance.
The facilities of "The Herald" Office for executing Book and Job Printing of every description are unequalled in Muskoka and Parry Sound. Our material is all new, and with the latest styles of type, good presses and skilful workmen, we are enabled to do work unsurpassed in Ontario. Orders from a distance receive prompt attention and forwarded free of postage.
F. T. GRAFFE & Co.
Publishers and Proprietors.

J. COOPER,

Hair Dressing and Shaving Parlor.

Opposite Queen's Hotel,

Canoes and Guides Furnished to Tourists.

BRACEBRIDGE MEAT MARKET,

H. McFARLIN, - Proprietor.

Prime Beef, Mutton, &c., Always on Hand.

Dominion Street,

OPPOSITE THE FIRE BELL.

BOWYER'S

Saddlery, Collar and Harness Depot

Manitoba Street,

BRACEBRIDGE, - ONTARIO.

WILLIAM BURTON,

TAILOR, &c.

Gents' Clothing Made in Latest Fashions.

A perfect fit guaranteed.

DOMINION STREET, BRACEBRIDGE.

D. B. LOWE'S

Bakery and Eating House.

Buns, Biscuits, Wedding Cakes.

MANITOBA STREET, BRACEBRIDGE.

LIVERY STABLE.

Daily Stage between Bracebridge and Baysville, connecting with steamer "Dean" on Trading Lake. Mail semi-weekly—Tuesdays and Saturdays.

JAMES LANGDON, Proprietor.

W. REAR, M. D.,

Physician and Coroner.

Residence and Office: Dominion Street,

OPP. CANADA METHODIST PARSONAGE.

Ontario Boot and Shoe Store,

Opposite Dominion Hotel,

JOHN SMITH, Proprietor.

Only first-class workmen employed.
Charges moderate.

JAMES LANGDON,

AUCTIONEER,

Butcher and Cattle Dealer.

Orders from private families delivered to any part of the village with promptness.

BRACEBRIDGE BUSINESS CARDS—[Continued].

The Old Established Waggon Shop,

JOHN GLOVER, Proprietor.

Waggons, Buggies, Sleighs and Cutters

Manufactured at shortest notice. Repairs neatly executed,

REAR HUBER'S BOOK & VARIETY STORE.

The Old Reliable Shaving Saloon,

Opposite Telegraph Office,

Where you can get as good work done in the Tonsorial line as you can get in Ontario. Also Pipes, Tobaccoes, Cigars of all brands. Oysters in season, Ice Cream in summer, wholesale and retail. Call and see them.

G. A. LINYON, Proprietor.

S. H. ARMSTRONG,

Wholesale and Retail Butcher,

Orders from private families promptly attended to.

BANK BUILDINGS, MANITOBA STREET.

KINSEY'S

Harness Emporium and Trunk Depot.

Harness, single and double, Riding Saddles for ladies and gentlemen. Trunks and Valises always in stock or made to order; Collars a specialty. A perfect fit guaranteed. Opposite Montreal Telegraph Office,

---

DAVID LAGACE,

Boot and Shoe Maker.

Manitoba Street, near Queen's Hotel.

All work executed under the personal superintendence of the proprietor.

S. E. BRACHER,

Dealer in

Groceries & Provisions,

PATENT MEDICINES. &c.

PETER M. SHANNON,

Agent for

London and Ontario Investment Company

(Limited.)

Money to Loan from 2 to 20 years at 8 per cent.

Also agent for Haggert Bros., Brampton, Agricultural Implements. Commissioner in Q. B. for taking affidavits. Issuer of Marriage Licenses, &c.

Atlas of Free Grant District of Muskoka and Parry Sound.

Price of Atlas $5.50; Single Maps 50c.; Single Views 25c. Sent post free on receipt of price. For sale at Isaac Huber's book and variety store, Bracebridge, or John Rogers, Port Carling P. O.

HUNTSVILLE BUSINESS CARDS.

TORONTO AND NIPISSING HOTEL,

THOS. BIRTCH, Proprietor.

Good Accommodation

For travellers, tourists and land seekers. Good Sample Rooms.

JOHN S. SCARLETT,

GENERAL MERCHANT.

Commissioner in Q. B., Issuer of Marriage Licenses. Eighty five good farms for sale. Settlers call or write and get prices and terms.

JOSEPH G. RUMSEY,

CONVEYANCER,

Auctioneer and Commission Merchant.

Commissioner in B. R. for taking affidavits, Cancellations and Locations effected, Patents obtained and Debts collected. Choice farm and village lots to be let or sold on easy terms. Office and residence, P. O. Building,

HUNTSVILLE, - ONTARIO.

DANIELS & MAY,

Dealers in

Shelf and Heavy Hardware,

Wholesale and Retail.

HUNTSVILLE AND BRACEBRIDGE.

ROBT. PHILLIPS,

General Commission Agent

And Conveyancer,

Farms Sold or Let on Commission.

POST OFFICE STORE.

J. E. KINTON,

Dealer in

Groceries, Dry Goods,

PROVISIONS,

BOOTS, SHOES, &c.

THE "FORESTER."

Published every Friday in Huntsville, situated in the heart of the free grant district of Ontario, has the widest circulation, giving the most faithful reports of the progress of the settlers and resources of the district; is the best medium of information for intending immigrants, and affords the greatest advantages to advertisers of any paper published in the district.

F. W. HOWLAND,   F. W. CLEARWATER & CO.
Editor.   Publishers.

HUNTSVILLE SAW MILLS.

E. AMBLER,

Proprietor.

All Kinds of Lumber

Always on hand.

VERY LOW PRICES.

THE QUEEN'S HOTEL,

JOHN PAGE, Proprietor.

THE FINEST LIQUORS AND CIGARS,

Billiard Room. Good Sample Roooms for Travellers,

G. T. DUNCAN,

Harness, Saddles, Whips

And all Horse Furnishings on hand.

STEAMER "NORTHERN."

Running between

Port Vernon & Port Sydney

On Mary, Fairy and Vernon Lakes.

DENTON & SMILEY, Proprietors,

REECE & McDONALD BROS.

General Store.

HUNTSVILLE AND KATRINE.

BERNARD PHILLIPS,

General Estate and Commission Agent.

Clerk of the 3rd Division Court,

HUNTSVILLE, - ONTARIO.

MISCELLANEOUS BUSINESS CARDS.

H. G. LADELL,

Dealer in

Dry Goods, Groceries, Provisions,

Crockery, Glassware, &c.

PORT SYDNEY STORE AND POST OFFICE.
[*See Illustration.*]

SYDNEY HOTEL,

W. H. MORGAN, - Proprietor.

PORT SYDNEY.

Situated on Mary Lake. Good accommodation for tourists. [See Illustration.]

R. SCARLETT,

GENERAL MERCHANT,

Dry Goods, Groceries, Hardware, General Merchandise, and Issuer of Marriage Licenses.

UTTERSON, - - ONTARIO.

ATLAS OF
Muskoka and Parry Sound.

Copies of the Atlas or any portion thereof, may be had on application to Isaac Huber, Bracebridge, H. R. Page & Co., P. O. Box 465, Toronto, or to John Rogers, Port Carling. Price of Atlas $5.50; maps, 50 cents each; illustrations, 25 cents each. Post free.

W. E. HAMILTON, B. A., T. C. D.,

BRACEBRIDGE, MUSKOKA.

Author of the description of Muskoka and Parry Sound in "The Undeveloped Portions of Ontario."

IMMIGRATION AGENT

For Ontario Government.

Information given to intending settlers, landseekers and investors on receipt of stamped envelope for reply.
Will shortly be published: "Facts about Muskoka," by W. E. Hamilton, B. A., T. C. D., and "Settlers' Testimony about Muskoka," collected by W. E. Hamilton, B. A., T. C. D.

JAMES MEDILL,

KATRINE.

Dealer in Dry Goods, Groceries,

Boots, Shoes, China, Glassware and Earthenware. Provisions a specialty.

S. R. G. PENSON,

General Draughtsman.

Finished drawings made from rough sketches. Maps, plans, etc., drawn and lithographed on the shortest notice.

402 YONGE STREET, TORONTO.

POLAR STAR HOTEL,

J. W. THOMAS, - Proprietor.

PORT CARLING.

Contiguous to Lakes Muskoka, Rosseau, Joseph, and smaller Lakes.

Splendid Fishing Grounds.

BOATS AND GUIDES.

Port Carling is one of the daily ports of call for Mr. Cockburn's steamers.

STEAM YACHT.

A small Steam Yacht can be chartered for tourist and fishing parties on very reasonable terms. Apply to J. W. Thomas, Polar Star Hotel, or to John Rogers, Port Carling P. O.

GEORGE B. BESLEY,

PORT CARLING.

Mill Owner and General Store Keeper.

All kinds of Sawed Lumber in stock.

GRAVENHURST BUSINESS CARDS.

EMPIRE

MUTUAL

Fire Insurance Company

OF ONTARIO.

Head Office:
No. 26 Wellington Street East,
TORONTO.

President, - - JAMES BURNS, Esq.
Vice-President, - W. E. CORNELL, Esq.
Manager and Secretary, - A. T. WOOD.
Bankers, - - BANK OF TORONTO.
Solicitors, - - FOSTER & CLARK.

Economy at the Head Office has a great deal to do with the success of an Insurance Company. The running expenses of the EMPIRE are very light when compared with other Companies, and it is our sole aim to give the public the benefit of a cheap insurance, and at the same time good security.

J. P. COCKBURN, Agent.
Gravenhurst.

A. COCKBURN & CO.,

GRAVENHURST.

GENERAL MERCHANTS.

Settlers, Lumbermen and Tourists Supplied at the

Lowest Going Prices.

J. E. CLIPSHAM,

General Blacksmith and

CARRIAGE BUILDER.

Special attention paid to Horse Shoeing.

PHILIP BARTHOLOMEW,

General Merchant.

Dry Goods, Groceries,

Hardware at lowest prices.

GRAVENHURST. - ONTARIO.

L. LOVE,

Blacksmith and Carriage Builder.

Buggies, Waggons, Cutters and Sleighs always on hand or made to order. Horse Shoeing a Specialty. All work guaranteed.

PARRY HARBOR BUSINESS CARDS.

THE GUELPH LUMBER CO.
(Limited.)

Wholesale Manufacturers of all kinds of

Sawn Lumber, Planed Lumber, Shingles,

LATHS, &c., &c.

DEALERS IN GENERAL DRY GOODS,

Ready-Made Clothing, Boots and Shoes, Groceries, Provisions, Hardware, &c.

THE THOMSON HOUSE.

ROBERT THOMSON, - Proprietor.

PARRY HARBOR, PARRY SOUND.

This hotel is conveniently situated, and commands an extensive view of the Sound. Parties visiting Parry Harbor or Parry Sound on business or pleasure will find that every attention is paid to the comfort of guests. Free 'Bus to and from the Steamers. Stage for the North in connection.

GOOD FISHING AND HUNTING.

THE McKEE HOUSE.

The first-class hotel of the District, commanding a splendid view of Georgian Bay, and in the neighborhood of the best fishing grounds on the lakes.

Good Accommodation for Sportsmen, Tourists and Commercial Travellers.

Separate sitting rooms and entrance for ladies. Montreal Telegraph Office. All steamboats call at wharf close to house.

JOHN McKEE, - - - Proprietor.

JAMES FORSYTH,

GENERAL BLACKSMITH.

Horse-shoeing a specialty.

All Kinds of Smith's Work

Done in a satisfactory manner.

CARRIAGE AND WAGGON
MANUFACTORY,

PARRY HARBOR.

The undersigned begs to inform the inhabitants of Muskoka and Parry Sound Districts that he is prepared to furnish them with a superior class of

Cutters, Sleighs, Buggies and Waggons.

Both light and heavy at reasonable terms.

FUNERALS ATTENDED TO.

Orders Solicited.

JAS. C. WHITCHELO,

VILLAGE LOTS

For sale in

PARRY HARBOR.

SEE PLAN, PAGE 42.

Apply to P. McCurry, or F. A. Foley, Court House, Parry Sound.

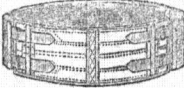

www.ingramcontent.com/pod-product-compliance
Lightning Source LLC
Chambersburg PA
CBHW030605270326
41927CB00007B/1049

9 7 8 3 7 4 1 1 1 8 8 4 5